SHADOW
LANDSCAPE

Also by Leslie Patten

Ghostwalker
Koda and the Wolves
The Wild Excellence
Biocircuits

SHADOW LANDSCAPE
Copyright © 2021 Leslie Patten

Published by Far Cry Publishing
Cody, WY
Lesliepattenbooks.com

ISBN: 978-0-578-89059-3

Cover design by Marina Jovic
Cover back photos by the author
Interior drawing of plane and pika by Marina Jovic
Interior drawing of bighorn sheep courtesy of Rock Art Stickers
All other interior drawings are in the Public Domain

Edited by Robert Macias

SHADOW
LANDSCAPE

STORIES FROM THE FIELD

LESLIE PATTEN

TABLE OF CONTENTS

PREFACE

Along a steep canyon corridor by my home, mountain goats graze the granitic precipices in winter. When not delicately perched on teacup ledges, they gather beside cliff edges, ready for quick getaways. On hikes to the canyon overlooks, I know the cliffs they prefer and bring my binoculars. I've learned to discern their warm white outline from the stark snow. At least, I could up until three years ago. About that time the goats seemed to disappear. They weren't wiped out by hunters or disease; they simply moved into what the goats considered more desirable territory. I asked a neighbor who is a long-time outfitter for bighorn sheep if he'd been seeing goats. The bighorns tend to overwinter in the volcanic range of the Absarokas, farther west of where the goats had been. He affirmed that a few years back he was seeing more and more goats where he'd been taking clients for bighorns, so he began including mountain goats in his hunts. The ungulates were exploring a moveable landscape.

Meanwhile, unlike the goats that gather in small groups, their tufts of off-white easily visible against the grey rock, the solitary lynx had evaded biologists in the Greater Yellowstone who had been actively scouting for them for years. Even a track in the snow would be sufficient. No lynx showed themselves, but could a few be concealed in this ecosystem of twenty-two million acres, making a living on pockets of snowshoe hares? Cats living in a shrouded landscape.

Then there are the invisible landscapes, darker than shadows. Hunting for clues of suitable bighorn reintroduction habitat, researchers map petroglyphs. These ancient images on rocks are messages indicating where large herds of long-lost bighorns once leapt and scrambled.

In political landscapes where grizzlies live, the government counts bears using a complicated mathematic formula called the Chao 2 method. While grizzlies go about their business, planes search meadows and high talus slopes to tabulate their numbers. Solitary animals, king of the forests, they are not easy to spot. No one is really certain of their population numbers, but certainty is of the essence when it comes to the grizzly's future fortunes.

Wild animals have their patterns, their home ranges, their repetitive habits just like we do, but they are also fluid. Their lives are driven by finding food, safety, and weather patterns, but they also have the added stress of keeping a constant eye out for the most unpredictable animal—humans. Our human world has burgeoned so rapidly that it has completely consumed our earth. Wildness has receded into the shadows. Finding wildlife is akin to finding Waldo in a sea of human activity. And with less wildlife on the landscape, whole ecosystems collapsing, and extinctions becoming more common, our serendipitous encounters are vanishing too. Shadow Landscape recounts a few stories of my own animal meetings, some intentional, others unexpected, in the vanishing world of wildness.

The majority of the stories included were written during the COVID winter, some in Arizona and others in Wyoming. But the events occurred over several years. Having worked for many years with plants and animals, I now consider the animal world like a troupe of jazz dancers. Wildlife sway and move in response to each other. They anticipate their partner's next maneuver; they are creative in their calculations and read with expertise every gesture, smell, and sign on the land. Meanwhile, we humans sit on the dance-floor bench with only the two-step under our belt. We are bumbling and awkward in our participation. Loud, fast, self-absorbed. The connection between all these tales is my own clumsy attempt to touch nature's heart, to understand the ineffable, to reach beyond my grasp and feel like I too am learning to jazz dance.

Two of the stories in the first section, *Gil and the Bees* and *The World of Fungi*, come from my time living in the Bay Area. Of course, we can connect with the beauty and wonder around us even in our backyards. As a child, my love of nature began by wandering my Los Angeles backyard counting bird's nests every spring and admiring the differences in their eggs. Most of the other essays take place near my home in Wyoming, where some of the last large animals in North America have room to roam.

End of the Wild, section two, concentrates on human interference and our bumbling, as opposed to our wonder. Each story, from *Wolves in the Crosshairs* to *Killing Coyotes to Grow Deer* tells a personal experience of human intrusion into the natural daily lives of wild animals. Every incident directly and personally educated me as to how far humans are willing to go to dominate the landscape. *Bighorn's Gordian Knot* centers around a thorny issue I became aware of when writing *Ghostwalker*. Mountain lions, particularly in the southwest United States, were being cleared off mountain ranges in order to reintroduce bighorn sheep. The issue is complicated since bighorn sheep were on the brink of winking out. In this essay, I delve deeply into the bighorn's multitude of issues, why mountain lions are not a major factor, and what a reasonable step forward might be.

In Part II, I ask the questions: how will we protect our wildlife into the future? What is our relationship to wildness? What are we losing when we lose wild nature and what do wildlife need to go about their business sans our awkward dance?

Over the last several years, the attack on wildlife and public lands has become more strident. Pristine environments where sage grouse mate and long migration routes where elk, pronghorn, and deer escape extreme winters, are being sold off for oil and gas wells. Grizzly bears are under constant pressure to be delisted so they can be hunted. The war cry for wolf elimination is escalating. Noisier, bigger, off-road vehicles are ubiquitous. Extreme sports are the latest fad, muscling into critical terrain for bighorn sheep and wolverines. Pikas are losing their home to a warming environment.

Our time is running out. These stories are my own attempt to share what I love. Let us all press ahead to save what we love.

PART I
THE SHADOW LANDSCAPE

A Pika Visits

Over the summer I added a small pantry to my cabin. I racked my brain for years trying to figure out how to fit a washer/dryer unit somewhere in my tiny house. Cabins in the remote mountains of Wyoming come *as is,* which basically means the furniture is not worth the previous owner hauling it out. Built in the 1950s, my cabin was used for family summer retreats by the previous owners. The clothes washing system was a portable washing machine with the sun for the dryer. I'd never seen a portable washer before. The machine was on wheels with two long hoses—one hooked to the sink faucet, the other drained the excess water. At first, I was happy to use the portable, although it occupied lots of wall space in the kitchen. I set up a clothesline and dried everything in the summer sun. But once I was living here full time, this setup became awkward in winter. A friend suggested drying my clothes outside during the winter months, letting them freeze, then knocking off the ice. I preferred to take my clothes to the laundromat when I was in town.

Days in the winter are short and town is an hour away. Between my volunteer work at the natural history museum, errands, and the laundromat, I was having a hard time fitting it all in and returning before dark.

Then the inevitable happened. After several years of use, the old relic started to leak. Try as I might, I couldn't fix it, yet I endured its foibles and soldiered on with the machine. But the final insult was when I noticed my clothes weren't getting any cleaner. It was a subtle revelation, but when I looked harder, it was obvious they'd probably never been clean after a wash, ever. My son helped me load the antique into the back of the truck and off to the town dump.

The next summer I invested in a mud room that doubled as a pantry and washer/dryer space. I increased my home footprint by one hundred fifty square feet and made my life easier. My trusted carpenter, who I called the Viking because he was a giant of a man—muscular and blonde— excavated into the hillside and recessed the room into it, an old-fashioned smart practice of early homesteaders. The mud room was to become the back entrance. I helped the Viking create two back steps out of several large limestone slabs covered in orange lichen. The steps faced the southern sky. New growth on the exposed hillside was just beginning to push up late summer with weeds. I seeded with native grass, but it wouldn't take hold till the following spring.

Early October, I was finding piles of plant material neatly arranged on the new stone steps. The first pile looked like tiny green tomatoes with the stalks attached. Confused, I thought maybe I'd bought cherry tomatoes and dropped a few green ones on my way inside. I tossed the clippings out on the bare hillside dirt. The next morning the green tomatoes were back again on the step.

This continued for a few days, until one morning I glimpsed a small creature, about eight inches in length with tiny ears, gathering grass from the front lawn. Although it was a cold October morning, the lawn was still green, and this miniature bunny lookalike was working away during a time when my scurry of ground squirrels was hibernating. I knew this animal, yet I just couldn't place him. I took a few photos. Over the next few days, tomato plants appeared on the limestone steps by the back door, laid out perfectly to dry in the sun, then would disappear. The following day more vegetation arrived. Meanwhile, I figured out that my little visitor was a pika—a very unusual guest at 6,300 feet.

I've seen pikas many times, but always in talus slopes at 10,000 feet altitude. Pikas live in the windswept Beartooth mountains near my home, but most of my sightings were on backpack trips into remote wilderness in alpine or subalpine terrain. Pikas make their living in some of the toughest, high-elevation country of the West. Where cliffs and mountains are eroding into large boulders and millions of sharp and smooth stones, that is their usual home. In that jumble of rock debris, I'd hear their characteristic whistle-calls before I'd spot them. They are territorial, but live in groups for added protection, making their whistles as alerts for each other. Eagles, coyotes, but especially weasels are their biggest threats. They don't hibernate in that extreme cold, but make haystacks of native vegetation, drying them on the rocks for the long winter.

What I also knew about pikas was that their very existence is threatened by climate change. They once lived across North America, but as glaciers retreated, they also retreated upslope into high elevations and now are found only west of the Rocky Mountains. Interestingly, some pikas survive at lower elevations where deep caves provide a constant cool temperature. The American pika is very temperature sensitive; death can occur after

brief exposures to temperatures greater than 77.9° F. As our climate warms, pikas, who've ecologically adapted to year-round cold, have no farther up to go. So this pika, living at my back doorstep, was not only an unusual visitor but maybe a test of their altitude range.

I was curious what my new friend was eating. I looked around my bare hillside, wondering where the tomato plant came from. I hadn't noticed the plant before, but my wild friend sure did. *Solanum triflorum* was popping up as a weedy guest on the mound behind the new addition. *Solanum triflorum*, commonly known as small nightshade, is an edible relative of the common tomato. This pika knew what was edible and what wasn't, even with different plants from his native home range.

For all their tough living, pikas are incredibly cute. In fact, they are adorable. I was now seeing my little friend regularly. He was up with the sun and every morning he was either at my front or back steps, chewing on some grass. His haystacks were always on the same southern-facing limestone steps. Besides leafy greens, the pika also dried and stored grass seed heads. I also noticed a small hole at the corner of the steps leading under the house into the dirt crawlspace that the Viking forgot to fill. The pika was living there. As one set of dried goods was complete, he'd move them into storage under the cool of the crawlspace, then get to work on his next batch. He had dehydrating down to a science.

I became curious exactly what the pika might want to dry out. I know you aren't supposed to feed wildlife, but what could it hurt to try an experiment with this little pika? What a rare opportunity. I started with lettuce. I'd place a few leaves on the step, then keep my eye on them. The pika would rearrange the leaves in what he thought would be the best drying position, or he might take some of them to his cavern below, which I assumed he was eating right away. From my non-scientific testing, he liked lettuce, carrot tops (but of course, he's in the rabbit family), kale; but he didn't care for arugula or radish sprouts, those spicy vegetables.

The pika stayed active all through the month of October. I wondered where he came from, how he got to my house. There were no other pikas here. They don't live at 6,300 feet and my home isn't the right habitat. I spoke with friends at the natural history museum in town where I volunteer. Was this a good sign? Could pikas adapt to lower elevations? We all worried together about this little lagomorph. Will he make it through the winter?

On October 31, the last day of general deer hunting season, a friend visited. He had an unfilled tag and we decided to go out together looking for a nice buck. I'd help him haul the deer if he was lucky. Winter was setting in and the temperatures were dropping with a light snow. Gary had permission from a neighbor to hunt on their private land. We headed out, and he shot a young buck. I helped him gut and load the buck into the truck bed. As we were returning to the cabin, rounding up the driveway, we spotted a short-tailed weasel, sometimes called an ermine. Still in his dark summer coat, the ermine stood out against the white landscape. The agile weasel was sneaking around the woodpile. Mice and voles live there, both favorite foods of his. Ermines are voracious eaters. They are shaped like miniature dachshunds, with elongated bodies and short legs. Their small, sinuous, tubular bodies are ideal for searching out prey in burrows, tight spaces, and under snow. Being thin and lightweight means they don't retain heat well, and so need a lot of calories to stay alive and warm. Watch a weasel hunt and it's like watching a video game on high speed. They can turn corners in an instant, searching in and out of holes more quickly than you can keep an eye on them. In winter, ermines turn white, camouflaged against the snow. With a high metabolism, they are always on the hunt, and in rich hunting grounds they will cache food. I've watched ermines on several occasions wait until birds are just about to fledge, then pop in and rob the nest. They seem to know exactly when the nestlings are the fattest yet still vulnerable.

Weasels will pursue rabbits, and are the main foe of pikas. I've found weasels up at 10,000 feet and a friend of mine told me how he once saw a weasel snatch a pika. I worried. I was leaving for the month of November in just a few days. Without other pikas to help make whistle alerts, would my little pika survive?

For the next several days I didn't see my pika. I would lay out lettuce, but it just sat there. I talked with a biologist at the museum who told me that pikas are pretty good at outsmarting weasels so maybe he got away. I left for a month with no evidence of my pika around. That morning of our deer hunt was the last time I saw my little friend. While we'd been hunting deer, that ermine was hunting the pika.

I asked tracker and mammalogist Jim Halfpenny about the little pika and his probable demise.

"Being a lone pika at 6,300 feet, he probably had little chance of survival."

Photographer Dan Hartmann, who lives in Silver Gate, Montana, was working on a photographic book on pikas in the Beartooth Mountains. He had a theory about where my pika arrived from. In September after the tourists are gone, I like to drive to the nearby Beartooths. One morning in late September, I drove to Island Lake, parked and spent the day hiking around the picturesque alpine lake at 10,000 feet. Dan thought the pika might have hitched a ride under the hood back to my house, only forty-five minutes away. Unfortunately for my pika, he picked the wrong spot to warm himself. But I had to admire my little emigrant who set to work immediately drying food for the winter while finding a suitable dry burrow. It was a fatal choice for the pika, but a wonderful month for me.

GIL AND THE BEES

I'd been keeping bees for about a year while living in the Bay Area when my friend Linda called to tell me there was a swarm in her cul-de-sac. Could I come and collect it from her neighbor's tree? Never having done this before, I told her to call our local bee club. The club gave her Gil's number. Gil said he'd be there at dusk when the bees were cold, but he needed some equipment. I arrived as the sun was setting with a hive super, or bee box, and saw a man around eighty years old standing by a bush where the bees were clustered. Gil was a heavyset large man with a white flop of hair. His eyes twinkled when he introduced himself. He told me he'd been working with bees since he was ten years old, but no longer kept bees at his house. He just liked to go where the bees were and lend a hand to others. He wore no suit or gloves, and when I gave him the super, he just whisked the cluster of bees in with his bare hands. That was the beginning of our friendship.

Beekeepers are an unusually friendly lot. All the bee-keepers I've ever met will go the extra mile for you. A few months later I was having trouble with one of my hives. Still a beekeeping novice, I couldn't understand why there were so many male bees, or drones, populating my hive.

Every time I checked the hive, the drone population in-creased. This seemed like it had to be a bad sign. Male bees are good for only one thing—mating. Since the queen only mates once in her lifetime, a generous population of males is a burden on the hive. Males do no work and collect no nectar. They only eat what the female workers make. They can't sting and are bigger than the females. A hive will keep a few males around, especially in the spring and early summer, in case they need a new fertile queen, but clearly something was wrong here.

I remembered Gil had given me his phone number. I called and explained the situation.

"I think your queen is gone and you have a laying work-er. Workers can't lay fertile eggs so they all become drones. I think I know what to do, but call Taber and ask them."

Taber is a mail order company for queen bees. They rec-ommended a drastic method.

"You're probably going to lose your hive. But try this. It works once in every three tries. Buy a new queen, but don't insert her in the hive. If you put her directly in, the bees will kill her. They've been tricked into thinking this laying worker is their queen."

Bees can have only one queen per hive. If another is in-troduced, either artificially or by hatching, the two queens will fight to the death.

"At night, move all the bees in your hive to a new box at least fifty feet away. Make sure you brush all of them into these new boxes. Place the old boxes back in their original position. The next morning, insert the new queen. The laying worker is too heavy to fly back to the hive. But the bees *might* still reject the new queen. Try it. One in three chances it works are good odds."

This sounded like a lot of work, but the new experience would be fun. I called Gil and explained what Taber said. He immediately said he'd help me with the undertaking. When the new queen arrived, I called Gil and early evening, working under floodlights, we began the laborious process. I carried the boxes over to him; he shook the bees into the new supers. Then I carted the empties back and brought him the next super. About a half hour and several stings later, we were done. Although the experiment didn't work and I lost my hive, Gil and I had bonded.

The following fall I was ready to extract honey from my one remaining hive, but wasn't clear as to the process or where to find an extractor. Once again, I called Gil, who invited me to join him and his old friend Bob Kaufman. Bob owned an extractor and lived close. Bob kept a few hives that Gil liked to assist with. Gil never took any honey home; he just enjoyed being around the bees. Bob also brewed beer in his garage, so the extraction process always turned into a small party with his homemade beer. For the next several years, Bob, Gil, and I would gather during autumn in Bob's garage for an extraction party.

In order to prepare to extract, I had to steal some honey-laden supers from the hive. Beekeepers in the Bay Area of California don't have to feed sugar water in the winter, or bring their hives into the basement and seal them up. Instead, they can leave a few deep supers for the bees to feed on in the winter. A super is a generic name for a single hive box. Supers come shallow or deep. Deep supers are exactly that—about twice as deep as the shallow ones. Each su-

per has room for ten frames or combs. These frames hold the foundation, made of either plastic or wax, that the bees build their wax honeycomb cells on. Shallow supers are used for honey while deeps are used for the brood. This is mainly because when a shallow is full of honey it weighs about fifty pounds as opposed to one hundred pounds for a deep super. Imagine lifting that off the hive. Over the course of a few weeks before extraction, you have to make sure the queen is laying in a deep super set at the bottom while you get ready to take off the shallow supers above for extraction.

It's good to remove the supers on a warm fall day when the majority of the bees are out finding nectar. I was preparing to go to Bob's house that afternoon. I removed three supers and brought them into the house. Usually, I would bring them into the garage where it's cool and enclosed. There is less risk of the bees smelling the honey and swarming in. But today I brought them into the kitchen, and before I could take them to the garage, I received a phone call. I took the portable phone into another room while the supers sat on the kitchen island. The day was hot. September can be the hottest month in California, and the sliding glass doors were open with the screens pulled. I must have gotten lost in my phone conversation and forgotten about the bees, because within five minutes my twelve-year-old son came running in yelling "Mom, the kitchen is full of bees!" Sure enough, the entire kitchen was swarming with bees. They smelled the sweet scent of their honey and came searching for it, somehow getting in through the screen doors.

Keeping bees has lots of twists and turns, and as a beekeeper in training, I was always in need of advice. On a warm spring day, I checked my hive and discovered it was queenless. I had lost my other hive over the winter to mites. If I lost this one too, I'd have no honey this year. I called Gil and asked what to do.

"Tony, my son-in-law, and I went up last weekend to a place in Vacaville where they sell bees by the pound. Buy three pounds and you'll have honey by fall."

Gil wanted to come along with me, even though he had just gone with Tony the week before.

"Why do you want to go for such a long drive when you were just there last week?"

"I like the drive. Besides, it's interesting to see the bees and the setup they have, plus it would be fun to go with you."

But it turned out he was busy the following weekend. So I took a friend and we drove out to Vacaville, an hour and a half from the Bay Area. After an hour, we turned off the freeway and snaked along a narrow country road. Farmhouses and small cottages were hidden amongst the oaks. The address was so obscure, we had to double back several times looking for the dirt cut-off that led to Bee Happy Apiaries' driveway. A sign at the fork read: "Drive past white house and uphill to barn."

We reached the barn at the top of the rise where a long line of cars waited, engines running. As we waited our turn, a young man appeared and asked how many pounds of bees we wanted. Although I'd planned on only one hive worth of bees, on the spur of the moment, I decided to buy a second hive. Why not up my chances for honey this fall? Always good to have a second hive in case something goes wrong. I paid for two three-pound packages of bees. Each package came with one queen.

The line of cars moved slowly. As we sat waiting our turn for bees, I noticed a large barn to my left. The barn was an open-air metal Quonset-style building, stacked inside to the ceiling with hive boxes. Human worker bees scurried all over the property, filling packages and handing them off to customers in cars. Bees swarmed everywhere: around the stacked supers, in the barn, around the cars, and in the back of the trucks where supers were being loaded. A ditch by our idling car was filled with supers strewn haphazardly, blackened with a cloud of bees. My friend turned the motor off and we stepped out. A young, attractive dark-haired woman, wearing jeans and a plaid shirt with the sleeves rolled up, was handing bee packages to buyers and explaining the instructions. She had a thick Czech accent and talked animatedly. I imagined I was transported to a small European villa with a centuries-old tradition of beekeeping.

Finally, our turn came. The young man brought two boxes constructed of wire and wood. Each box was the size of a large shoebox. The top, bottom, and ends were made of wood, while the long sides were made of plastic mesh. An upside-down tin can covered a hole at the top. This housed the sugar water that fed the bees. A slit in the top of the wood by the tin can held a much smaller box, about the size of a matchbook and also made of wood and mesh. Inside this box was the queen.

"Put them out in the cool of the evening. Just pull off the feeder, slide the queen box out, and dump them all in the hive body. Use a shallow super."

I had brought my truck. Most vehicles in the line were cars.

"Is it alright to put these in the back of the truck? Will it be too windy?"

He didn't think so.

"These are for free," he said, referring to the freeloader bees that swarmed around the outside of the box's wire netting. There were hundreds of bees clinging to the outside of each box.

"They'll probably stay on there all the way back to the Bay Area."

The incessant humming of the bees, the swarms in the warm air, was like a heartbeat of life itself. I knew why Gil wanted to return with me. The whirling drone of bees has a strange calming effect, meditative and transportive.

The day was hot for mid-April and when I arrived home the truck bed was swarming with bees. The freeloaders had survived and were creating quite a ruckus in my cul-de-sac. A neighbor and her two kids walked over to ask me to vote "yes" on the local school bond. With the swirl of bees, she wanted to know what was going on around my truck. When I told her what I was doing, she pulled her kids out of the car and brought them over for a bee lesson. I took them inside the house and gave them some fresh honeycomb.

Even after I removed the two three-pounders from the truck bed, the freeloader bees still swarmed there. I drove to the Safeway parking lot for an errand. The bees accompanied me. I drove back home. The bees were still there. I wasn't sure why this was happening. Back at Bee Happy Apiaries, they told me that they just scooped up bees from hives and combined them with reared queens. That would mean these bees weren't even used to my new queen's pheromones.

My friend who'd accompanied me to the bee farm went home and returned with her teenage son. They wanted to watch the release that evening. My empty supers were ready with the three-pounders full of bees seated nearby. My guests kept their distance while I worked one box at a time. First, I pulled off the tin sugar can. The bees were balled up in the box keeping warm, maybe also imitating a swarm. I had to shake and shake the box in sharp, jerking motions in order to force the bees out of the three-inch circular hole and into my empty super. Later, my friend said she could barely see me through the masses of bees flying over my head. A strange primal power comes with shaking a ball of twelve thousand bees repeatedly with abandon. The vitality of the swarm produced a phenomenal pulsing in my body.

I completed the first box and moved on to the second. The tin can was stuck. I yanked several times, but couldn't release the can from the hole. I put my foot on the top of the wooden box and pulled the can with all my might. I repeated this over and over until, just when I thought I'd need a tool, the can released. I was nervous because bees dislike abrupt and sudden movements. I started shaking the bees into the empty super. But my fears were unfounded as the cool air rendered them docile. They easily slipped into the large hive box, no worse for wear because of all my pounding. Besides, these were Carniolans—honeybees bred for their gentleness—and they definitely exhibited that.

Finally, I hung the small box with the queen between two frames. I had placed pushpins in the side to hang it better. The idea is to allow the bees time to become used to the new queen, through her pheromones, so they will accept her. Two or three days are usually enough time. The people at the apiary told me to slip the queen into the hive body that evening. Prudence told me to use caution. If the bees didn't accept this queen, they'd destroy her. Two days later, I returned to the hives and pulled loose the small cork that confined the queen inside the box. The bees had chewed most of the cork away, trying to free her. She slid quietly down into the dark bowels of the hive.

I'd been checking on the bees fairly regularly and both queens seemed to be laying nicely. But a few weeks later I noticed one of the hives was weak: the laying pattern just wasn't right. I checked in another week and a half later and found no larvae or capped cells of larvae. That was how I knew this hive no longer had a queen. I had been watching the hives periodically from my office window and could tell that one had strong activity but the other much less. Yet finding no larvae came as a surprise. I immediately ordered a new queen by mail. My dilemma was this: It takes twenty-one days to grow a worker from an egg. Bees live for only three to six weeks in the summer. My three pounds (twelve thousand bees) were already declining and no new eggs were being laid. I had to obtain a queen, get the bees accustomed to that queen, and get that queen laying, plus have enough bees remaining to tend to the larvae and the queen before new bees hatched. It all seemed a close call. Who else to call but Bob and Gil?

"Don't worry 'bout that," said Gil. "You'll have time. I'm sorry I can't help you re-queen as I'm going on vacation."

Bob was more scientific.

"Too bad you already ordered a queen. What you could have done was take a frame of fresh brood from your other hive and put it in your queenless hive. The bees would make a queen."

I never thought of that. Such are the nuances of experienced beekeeping. Bees can sense they are queenless within hours and will start enlarging the cell around a larva that's no more than three days old. In my case, it appeared that no eggs were available to make a queen with.

"But you'd have to be sure there were fresh eggs in that frame. Do you know how to recognize eggs?"

I told him I didn't.

"You have to train your eye."

If a young egg or larva is present, the bees make a specially constructed cell and start feeding the larva royal jelly, a special food produced in the head glands of nurse bees. That food is what turns an otherwise common worker into a virgin queen. When the queen emerges, she must be the one and only. She kills all the other queen larvae and fights an old queen to the death if one exists. Within a few days, she leaves the hive for her first and last time to mate.

"But there are no drones in my young hive, so where would she find drones?"

After I asked this, I realized it was a stupid question. She only has to mate once in her lifetime, with probably fifteen to eighteen drones, or male bees. From the sperm of all these drones, she'll create a smorgasbord of genetic material. She wouldn't want to mate with her own genetic kind.

"The drones come. They're around and she goes to the place where they are."

Within a few days, my queen arrived by mail with a few attendants, some of whom died in transit. But she was intact. The wooden cage was identical to my previous ones, but this had a sugar plug instead of a cork. The sugar feeds the queen from the inside while the bees in the hive eat her out of the cage from the outside. I put her in a dark cupboard till I was ready the next day.

I was expecting a parent from my son's school to help with the re-queening. He had expressed interest in my bees when he saw them at a party in my home.

"I could do that. I have space in my backyard. Yeah, I could do that."

"Do you want to go in with me sometime?" I asked.

"What do you mean 'go in'?"

On several occasions he'd expressed interest and I kept offering to take him inside the hive. Curiously, he never seemed to understand what I meant. I think he thought the bees never needed watching or tending. Of course, in the days before mites, pre-1990, old-timers tell me that's almost how it was. Put on a few extra honey supers in the spring; take them off in the fall. But when the mites came from Europe, the bee population was decimated. They had no resistance whatsoever. Ninety percent of our wild honeybees were killed. Now commercial and hobbyist beekeepers need to pay much more attention. The method a lot of beekeepers used was to hang mite strips in their hives. Bob said he never used them. His idea was that the hives that survived would be genetically stronger. He used natural selection as his method and just dealt with the losses.

My friend never showed and I began re-queening without him. It took only a few moments and I left it for three days. When I returned, the bees had almost eaten her out of the box through the sugar plug, but she was still trapped inside. All the attendants were dead, but she looked very viable. Queens, unlike workers, live a long time, up to six years.

I carefully pulled the staples from the screen so as not to damage her. Worker bees crawled all around her and over my hands. They were anxious to get her inside now that they were used to her scent. Or, at least I hoped they were accepting of her. The workers could still kill her if they decided to.

My assignment was to come back in three or four days and look for eggs. Bob had drawn a picture for me of a comb cell with an egg inside. He neatly sketched a hexagon.

"It's not to scale," he told me, which made me chuckle because he had drawn the cell so large. He explained that the queen will lay the egg right in the middle of the bottom of the cell.

"It looks like a dot with a little tail. It's white and easy to see."

Worker bees that start laying will attach their egg to the side of the cell wall because their abdomen isn't long enough to insert all the way to the bottom. Like what happened to my hive, a laying worker will only produce sterile drones, and since drones do not work, the hive will eventually die.

I started beekeeping because of a mysterious arthritis that plagued me on and off for twenty years. Diagnosed as reactive arthritis, it affected tendons and other soft tissue in my hands and feet. I tried many natural remedies, but only cortisone injections seemed to help. During all these healing experiments, one of the more painful remedies I tried was bee therapy, which basically is sting therapy. The idea is to grab a bee with tweezers between the thorax and the abdomen, gently rub the tip of its abdomen on a pre-marked spot, and the bee will release its stinger onto that area. I became quite accomplished at stinging myself, though it's not really something to boast about. I'd mark the swollen areas with ink X's, grab a bee right off of a flower with my tweezers, and rub it on the X. Some people say to leave the stinger in until it dries up—maybe five to ten minutes—others swear that the first one to two minutes delivers all the venom. The stinger, including usually part of the bee's insides, sits on you and pulses away, pumping venom. The poor bee crawls off to die, its insides literally torn out. A bee in the field has nothing to defend and will almost always fly away if disturbed. I began feeling angst every time I had to kill one.

People who do a lot of stinging usually collect bees from a hive, then put them in a jar. The healing jar goes in a dark cool location and you feed them honey. I did this for a while too. One thing you notice is that the older the bee, the less likely it is to sting you. You can tell the older bees because they are darker in color and shinier as their hairs rub off. With an older bee I might sometimes have to push its abdomen over and over into my skin. This was definitely torturous, for the bee and me, because I kept expecting the sting that never came.

I was pretty much a coward. I could never get beyond five or six stings at a time, three times a week, for about six weeks. After this intensive therapy, I saw little difference in my arthritic sites. What I did notice was a sense of euphoria and energy that lasted for hours after the procedure. The body releases endorphins and cortisol in response to the venom, which in turn boosts the immune system.

I did come out of the treatment with an interest in beekeeping, however. I'm really a perpetual amateur. It's the experience of going into the hive that keeps captivating me. I found all the bee activity, the humming and buzzing, very neurologically calming. During the times I wasn't feeling well, I knew going into the hive for only fifteen minutes would be restorative. I'd forget my pain, become focused and calmed. Opening up a hive consumes one's conscious-ness. It takes focus, but it is more than that. Being in direct contact with fifty thousand bees, buzzing, humming, crawl-ing excitedly on your hands and around your face plunges you into an otherworldly experience. You crack the lid and pump a few puffs from your smoker into the top frames. Then wait a moment for the bees to forget their home in-vader. They will respond to the smoke by drinking honey. The bees believe their house is on fire and they will have to abandon it. They are readying themselves for what they believe will be their long flight looking for a new home. Watching all the activity, you forget to be afraid, even for-get these bees can sting. Sometimes I have to take the hive apart to access a deep super. That means I'm removing su-pers and placing them to my side, usually on top of an emp-ty super for support. I'm completely disrupting the bee hive. By the time I arrive at the bottommost super, thousands of bees are flying all around me.

I once took a workshop at the home of a man who kept over a hundred hives professionally. Only two of us showed up for the workshop. In the afternoon the man and his wife began opening up several hives at a time. The wife was working the hives in only shorts, a t-shirt, and a hood. Hundreds of thousands of bees flew around us as we searched deep into the bottoms of several hives at the same time. This man was moving and talking so fast I could barely keep up. He found a frame with lots of queen cells. He took that frame and put it in a weaker hive. Then, as he searched the frames, he found one with an emerging queen. We watched as the queen emerged from her pupae.

I asked his wife if she'd ever been badly stung since she was so scantily dressed.

"Only once. I was unloading hives from the back of a truck, when I dropped the hive box. That was bad. One time my daughter was badly stung and had to go to the hospital."

After that workshop, I stopped wearing gloves. The smell of the smoke from the smoker, prying off the frames, which the bees seal with propolis from tree resins, holding them up to inspect for honey and brood, watching the bees dive head first into the cells to drink up honey when threatened by the smoke, looking for drone cells and queen cells—there's always so much to do and observe, it forces a person to stay present.

Within a few days, I suit up to look for the eggs. I stoke the smoker, don my hood, and open the hive in question. Although I had two deep supers for the hive body, I know the queen will probably be in the bottom one. I briefly inspect the top box and find that it is all honey, so I pull the box off and go into the bottommost super. Queens usually like to lay in the middle frames within the box, while the honey to support the brood goes around the outside of the frame cells. When all ten frames are in the box, it's hard to inspect, so I pull off the end frame and set it gently down beside me. Then I head directly for one of the middle frames. I pry off the propolis and nudge the frame out of the box. I hold it to the light, yet I see nothing in the cells. I take the frame out of the shade of the tree where the hive body lay and walk into the sunlight. I look and look, but through the netting of the hood I can't distinguish any eggs. The white plastic of the frame just shines back at me, making it that much harder to see white eggs.

"I don't think you'll see eggs. I can't," Gil would later tell me. "Bob has good eyes."

I repeat this procedure with the next frame. Still no luck. By the third frame I'm getting nervous. Have I lost my queen? I hope they haven't killed her. I decide to remain still and give the bees and the cells a harder look. I watch the bees busily moving around and over the cells. They are all workers, no drones. All the movement fascinates me and I'm mesmerized. Suddenly, I see her. The queen. She is unmistakable. I've never found a queen before in my hives. With a full and active hive, she is hard to spot and most beekeepers only see her on occasion, if at all. But there she is, so much larger than the other bees, and much fatter than just a few days ago. Her abdomen is swollen with eggs. I watch her for a while. She appears oddly vulnerable and I want to put the frame back in the hive. I step toward the hive and she disappears into the mass of bees on the frame. I feel I need to keep her in view as I walk back to the hive in order to make sure she's safe. I look for her again, remembering what Bob had told me: "I didn't used to be able to see her. At the demonstration hive at the county fair, my wife could always spot her, but I never could. When I asked her how she did it, she said it was so easy because she looks so different. Not just bigger. The secret is that she's shiny... shinier than all the other bees. She lives a long time and all the other bees keep rubbing her. Eventually they rub off all those hairs on her thorax and abdomen and she's just shiny."

I am elated. I put the frame gently back so as not to hurt her, close up the box, and go inside to call Bob.

"I saw her."

"Wow, you actually saw her."

"I did."

"You know what that means? They've accepted her. She'll be laying now. Did you see the eggs?"

"No. I looked and looked but couldn't see them."

"You'll just have to train your eye. It's easy. You'll just have to train your eye."

A few weeks after my trip to Bee Happy Apiaries, I had a busy day meeting with new clients. Gil's wife had recently called. I didn't know Dodie, had never met her, but she wanted to discuss a front yard remodel. Gil would be my last stop for the day.

When I arrived around 6 p.m., Gil met me on the front steps of their modest home in a nice neighborhood, I assumed he and his wife of fifty-two years had lived here a long time. Dodie had obviously been a beautiful woman in years past. Tall and slender, she didn't look even close to her age. She kept a formal but friendly emotional distance. Her demeanor became clearer as the conversation about plants progressed. Gil, on the other hand, kept engaging me, joking, always a twinkle in his eye. He had no intention of taking any of this too seriously. We three stood in the front yard while Dodie explained precisely what she wanted done. Two large eucalyptuses framed the house. We discussed their desire for low maintenance, the existing drainage, where to hook up the sprinkler system.

"We won't be here for long," Gil said.

I paused. I tried not to think the unthinkable, so I said what I usually say in my job to a statement like that: "You're thinking about moving?"

"I have the cancer. Nothing they can do about it. Doctor says two, maybe three more years. All he can do is make me comfortable. When I go, I'm sure Dodie will want to sell the place."

He said it in a way that was more than matter-of-fact. It was an acceptance. Dodie didn't wince. I wanted to ask what kind of cancer, but I looked at her and just couldn't. It was apparent she wanted to keep our interaction formal. I said nothing. The conversation skipped a beat. Caught between Dodie's need for formality and my angst over Gil's revelation, I struggled to find the right approach. I allowed my work manner to take charge. It became easier to forget than to remember. We finished up our arrangements.

"How long before you have a plan?" Dodie asked.

"At least two months before I can begin. I'm swamped right now."

"That's good. We've waited this long; we can wait some more. The fellow who did the back yard told us six months. We have a friend whose daughter could do it. She came out here to look at it. I decided, though, that it wouldn't work with her. We're not friends."

I looked at her. "Oh," I said, not understanding her statement but acting like I did.

"No, I mean, you and me. We're not friends."

"Oh," I said again. I understood that's how she wanted it.

By the time my design was completed, and my crew was doing the installation, Gil was gone. Dodie had called to tell me while I was grocery shopping. Unfortunately, it was after his funeral. All I could say was how happy I was to get to know Gil. He was a bright light, always with that twinkle in his eye, never missing an opportunity to help friends and strangers because he enjoyed the bees and the company. Sometimes when I think of Gil, I imagine a man who was shaped by that celestial racket of bees. I envision him working with bees as a ten-year-old boy, his consciousness honed to their otherworldly voices. I think of the man who loved to go into the hive, becoming attuned to their droning noise, forgetting himself, soaking up their sermon, then going about his usual day. By the end of his life, the bees and their music had transformed him. He was a gentle, loving spirit; and like the darkened, older bees in my healing jar, he had to be coaxed hard to deliver a sting. It was so much easier to twinkle than to sting.

DICKINSON PARK

I wrote this story in 2004. I was living in the Bay Area and arranged to meet two friends for a week-long backpack of The Beaten Path in the Montana Beartooths. The plan was to have my friends fly into Billings, while I drove with our gear and two dogs—my golden retriever Soona and my friend's border collie Merlin. The story begins after our backpack ends and I'm returning to California. I decide to make one last solo short trip to the eastern side of the Wind River Mountains in Wyoming.

By the time I arrived in Lander, it was after one o'clock. The drive from Cody to Lander passes through the Wind River Canyon, a 2,500-foot-deep canyon. The highway winds through the canyon along the left side of the broad river; the railroad tracks hug the hillside on the opposite bank. The road is a consistent gradient, passing signs with geological time periods of the rock dating back to Precambrian. This is, after all, dinosaur country. The river, always to the right and below the road, has this strange appearance of defying gravity and traveling uphill. Obviously, an optical illusion, due in part to the uplifted sedimentary rock. I had to stop and see this for myself. I found a turnout and walked down to the river. A British tourist and his son were also contemplating this strange phenomenon. I let the dogs swim and drink while we discussed the weird sensation of watching a river flow uphill.

When I arrived in Lander, I immediately headed for the Forest Service ranger station to obtain my permit. A sign at the entrance walkway said to use the other door. The main one was "closed due to construction" and "Do not walk on the grass. We don't walk on yours!" I followed the detour signs, but they only led me in circles around the building and back to where I started. I walked around a second time and a third time looking for an entrance but couldn't find one. Finally, I decided the office was vacant. The bulletin board outside said to call Tony for information about Dickinson Creek trailhead.

I found a pay phone down the street at the gas station and called the number for Tony. It rang and rang. A nearby convenience store was the next logical place to inquire. I directed my question to a young woman behind the counter.

"Do you know what's happening at Dickinson Creek?"

She looked puzzled. A fit, sandy-haired man who'd been stocking shelves heard my query and walked over.

"That's been closed all summer," he said. "Been some kind of dispute between the Shoshones and the Forest Service. The Indians haven't let anyone pass through the reservation. Made quite a few folks around here mad. Lots of people like to use that area for fishing and camping."

"But…why? Are you sure it's still closed?"

"Guess the rangers just wanted to have too much control. The Indians didn't like that and demonstrated they have clout too. I'm sure it's still closed. Why don't you go to the Sinks? That's nice too."

He was referring to the Sinks Canyon State Park. Nine miles from town, Sinks Canyon is popular with rock climbers for its dolomite, sandstone, and granite cliffs. I was afraid it would be crowded. Besides, somewhere along that road was where Amy Bechtel disappeared in 1997 without a trace.

I was here that year. It was my first return trip to the Wind River range since the 1970s. I was in Jackson with friends and my eight-year-old son. I'd wanted to return to the Winds for over twenty years. My friends agreed to take my son with them to California while I spent five days camping out of the Big Sandy trailhead. Big Sandy is near the southwestern edge of the Wind Rivers. It bears the distinction of being the most remote and isolated trailhead in the Wind Rivers, a long lonely drive through a maze of dirt roads. Twenty-five miles from any paved road, the gravel roads travel through desert country, until they reach the foothills. The last ten miles are some of the worst roads on the western side of the Winds, potholed and rutted. In the mid-1990s, Big Sandy was popular primarily with experienced climbers, locals, and a few backpackers. I chose that trailhead because although it's a long drive, it's an easy five miles to the lake. I'd had a series of back injuries, and this was my first time backpacking in many years. I wanted to test my limits, but on an easy trail into the high country.

Two days before I left the Jackson area for Big Sandy, the local newspapers were full of articles about Amy, who lived in Lander. Amy had driven her car along the Loop Road, which passed by the Sinks, for a quick run. Fit and athletic, she was scoping the trail for an upcoming track meet. When she didn't come home, teams of search parties combed the area. They never found her body, blood, hair, tracks, or any other clues. One footprint was all that remained and even that was partially erased. A few years ago, a fisherman found a Timex Ironman watch like the one Amy was wearing when she disappeared. But apparently those are fairly common watches and there was no evidence to indicate that the watch belonged to her.

At first her husband was a suspect, but his alibi was airtight. He had been rock climbing with a friend. The case is still unsolved. That summer, hiking alone, I was looking over my shoulder the first three miles. I reasoned that anyone who was a serious abductor wouldn't venture farther than that. Of course, this was my own fabrication, but it seemed logical. Amy's abduction in the Winds, not many miles away, was unsettling during my entire backpack. So it wasn't surprising that even seven years later, the memory still haunted me. I didn't feel like going alone close to where Amy disappeared.

"I'm sure it's still closed and will be for the rest of the summer. If you want to be certain, go across the street and ask at the fishing and camping store. They'll know."

The tackle shop had a sign taped to the counter: *Dickinson Creek now open as of Wednesday, August 18. Permit required.*

"Just opened two days ago." The woman in her fifties behind the counter was short, slightly plump, and to the point. Although she didn't seem like the camping type, every clerk kept interrupting her to ask questions about fishing, special tackle, hunting, or camping spots. She was the reservoir of all things terrain related.

"People are irked. You didn't used to need a permit for Dickinson, but you do now. You gonna fish?"

"No."

"Doesn't matter. You still need a fishing license. Each day you are on Indian land you need a fishing license. Since you cross their land twice to get in and out, you need a two-day permit. I need to know your exact itinerary so I can write down the days."

This was annoying. I didn't mind paying, but I didn't want to be tied to a schedule. What if it rained? What if I wanted to stay longer? I asked what might happen if I didn't follow the scheduled days for crossing the reservation.

"I have no idea. The Shoshones will probably have some guards out though."

"Is the turn-off through Fort Wa-sha'-key?" I asked, placing emphasis on the second syllable.

A man behind the counter suddenly turned and looked at me.

"Let me just save you the embarrassment right now," he said curtly. "It's Fort *Wash*'-sha-key. Just think of washing the key, and you got it. And it ain't Popo AH'-gee. Its' Poe-Poe-Zhuh. Those Indian names can trick your tongue."

I paid for the permit for three days and left for Fort Washakie, gateway to the Wind River range and Wind River Reservation.

The dirt road up the mountain from town is twenty miles long. I had to take it slow, driving over an hour to reach the high meadows of Dickinson Creek campground and trailhead. The 4,000-foot elevation change and switchbacks keep you slightly queasy, feeling as if you're leaning off the mountain's edge. About halfway, I stopped for some Native children learning how to drive cattle overflowing onto the road. My dogs were barking in the back of the truck while the parents gave their kids instructions.

It was almost five o'clock when I reached the trailhead. The light was closing in on me. I could barely find the parking area. Not a soul had been there all summer, and the campground was deserted and overgrown with weeds. It was crude, without water, yet had clear designated sites. A large open meadow, the size of a few football fields surrounded by pines and spruce, glowed rustic brown in the light of the retiring sun. I got out my guidebook and debated what to do. The book said that there were no campsites along the trail till the lake, six miles in. Soona was limping and with only a few hours of light left, I decided to stay put, and camp in the campground, yet I didn't like that choice. I'm always leery of trailhead campgrounds, especially after the Amy Bechtel incident, and this one had been deserted all summer. So was the backcountry. Having talked with several people in town, it appeared no one knew the trailhead was even open. But I seemed to have no choice.

I picked a wooded site next to the meadow, and decided not to set up my tent. Although someone had collected wood already, I was too tired to build a fire. I formulated a plan. Rain was predicted for the day after next, so I decided to forget backpacking, and just hike the twelve miles as a day hike. I would get up early, pack up, and begin around seven. I could be out by four or five, and drive the lonely dirt road back to Fort Washakie while it was still light.

I made dinner and walked into the meadow to eat where there were fewer mosquitoes. The dogs seemed nervous and jumpy, barking at the wind or the shadows on the rocks. Maybe it was because I was nervous. I've camped alone a lot, but this was the loneliest spot I've ever been. No humans had been here for a long time, and it felt like that. The wild had taken over. I thought about my hike tomorrow by myself—how not a soul would be around if something happened to me. My mind wandered to an incident that occurred a few days before in the Beartooths where I'd spent the previous week backpacking with friends from California.

It had been storming all day and we were camped at timberline. The decision was made to descend to a lower elevation for more protection. When we arrived at Rainbow Lake meadows, the three of us were drenched and cold. Because so many backpackers were seeking refuge from the lightning storms at the higher elevations, it was hard to find a decent campsite. Our clearing was small and had no fire pit. Three women camping nearby offered to share their fire so we could dry out our boots. Maggie was originally from Colorado, but she had worked in Utah for several years before taking a job in the teachers' union in Montana. Her two friends were from Chicago and they'd all joined up for a week of adventure backpacking. As I sat on the log warming myself and drinking tea, Maggie's friend Louise couldn't stop moving and feeding the fire. About every fifteen minutes she'd disappear, only to return with a huge ten-foot fir branch that she placed stump-end into the fire. Within a few minutes, our small fire turned into a bonfire. When the wet logs started to smolder, Louise worried aloud, disappeared, and then reappeared with more tree limbs. The ranger came over at one point and, to my surprise, was completely untroubled about our huge blaze. While Louise exercised her pyromaniac tendencies, Maggie entertained us with conversation and stories. She was the lively and charismatic one of the group. I asked her questions about her job and what it was like to live in Montana.

"Lots of freemen up here. Montana's got to be the only state where the population has actually declined."

"What's a freeman," I asked.

"Well, have you ever heard of the story of Kari Swenson? Biggest story in Montana in the last twenty years. It was even made into a TV movie."

I got comfortable on my log, ready for a good yarn.

"Kari was a world class athlete. One day she went running in the Gallatin Wilderness, not far from here. She was training for the U.S. Olympic team. Two mountain men—a father and his son—abducted her. The father told Kari he needed a wife for his son. Imagine that! The two men tied her wrist with a rope and dragged her through the backcountry. They were living free, out of bounds of society, and doing whatever they wanted. At least, that's how they looked at it. They were free men."

"A search party was organized when Kari didn't return home. A friend of hers joined the search party to look for her. He was a good tracker, and came across where they had sequestered her. When he approached, the two men shot and killed him. When Kari tried to warn the searchers to stay away, they shot her in the chest too. And although she wasn't dead, she pretended to be. The men freaked out and ran away, leaving Kari half-dead. She crawled over to a dropped pack and sipped water, keeping herself hydrated. Somehow she survived, and a few hours later a helicopter rescued her. She still lives in Bozeman."

"What happened to the men?"

"They escaped into the woods. For almost a year there was a manhunt looking for them. One day a hunter ran into them cooking squirrel in the backcountry. They asked him about Kari, saying they had heard about the story. When

the hunter told them she was alive, they looked visibly relieved. That tipped him off and he called the sheriff. That
was the end for them. But Montana got its two hours of TV
fame. Didn't you ever see that movie?"

I mentioned the Amy Bechtel story to Maggie and told
her I was in Jackson when that occurred.

"I know about that one too. Never did figure out what
happened to her. Guess there's not too much to do up here
and I kind of follow those stories. Anyway, that's what a freeman is. They don't believe in the rules of society. They make
their own rules. We've got lots of them up here in Montana,
and they keep moving in while everyone else is moving out."

"Interesting that both were runners and top athletes,"
I said.

"Maybe that was what made them attractive to these
mountain men. You know, fit women!"

The thought of that story now made me shudder. I
didn't really think there were crazy freemen up here on the
Reservation, but my mind kept wandering back to those
stories of Kari and Amy, alone in the mountains, trusting,
empowered by their athletic prowess.

Something was moving in the meadow about 500 yards
away. I went back for my binoculars. It was a bull moose.
I edged closer and checked the wind. We were downwind.
Merlin spotted it but he stayed close, at attention. After a
while Soona saw it too and began a low growl. "Quiet," I told
her. After a half hour, the moose went to bed down in the
woods as the sun angled below the horizon. With nothing
to do and the intention of getting up early, I tied the dogs up
and got into my sleeping bag.

At about 9:30 p.m., I was awakened by the sounds of
screaming coming from the forest. It was a cacophony of

many voices. The locus was within a few hundred feet of my camp, but seemed to reverberate throughout the entire meadow. I woke scared. To my sleepy ears it sounded like screaming banshees.

Banshees are female spirits in Irish Celtic lore. The wailing and screaming of the banshees foretold of a coming death to whomever heard it. But the spirit is cross-cultural. Naturalist and author Jim Corbett, who grew up in the Kumaon hills in the Himalayan foothills, used to tell stories about banshees there called churails. As a child, Corbett roamed the nearby jungles. He became a highly skilled tracker, learning the animal signs, and able to recognize every bird call. A churail, Corbett says, is the most feared of spirits in the forest. She appears in the form of a woman and mesmerizes her victims. Corbett had many supernatural experiences throughout his life in the jungles of India. One evening at his home in Kaladhungi, during dinner on the veranda, he heard the call of the churail, a screaming, eerie sound coming from a haldu tree. Using binoculars, Corbett saw a bird he had never seen before about the size of a golden eagle. Another time he heard "the scream of a human being in mortal agony," although the shriek came from a village he knew was deserted.

Corbett rightly points out in his book *Jungle Lore* that we humans are children of the daylight, adapted to the light. But when "daylight fades and night engulfs us, our sense of sight we depended on no longer sustains us and we are at the mercy of our imagination." This was my predicament at Dickinson Park.

Although I'd never heard banshees, it seems I knew exactly what they might sound like and at this very moment they were running in the fields by me. These were not howls, like coyotes or dogs. I listened. They were high-pitched, almost laughing noises. I fumbled for my flashlight and pointed it at the dogs. They sat attentive, unafraid, listening, interested. Maybe these banshees were coming out of their dens to hunt for the night. I didn't imagine a woman, but my mind's eye envisioned spirit hounds roaming the night, shrieking. The sounds echoed through the meadow and soon went off into the distant forest. In a few moments, all was quiet again.

I had an unsettling sleep, afraid of the darkness, afraid of what might have taken Kari Swenson in Big Sky or Amy Bechtel in the Sinks, afraid of being isolated at this trailhead. I was glad the dogs were by my side.

At three a.m. I was awakened again. I heard the bull moose first. He made a few loud and low sounds like a snort and a honk. The banshees were making another pass, returning to their dens after their hunt. Their strange singing noises, screeching, rolling through octaves, up and down alien scales, drove me silent inside. Again, I watched the dogs with my headlamp. And again, their ears pricked up, listening attentively. Like the incessant howling of a wind that suddenly pauses, the sounds stopped.

I lay in the dark for a while, waiting for sleep. The dogs had settled down. I heard a faint noise that resembled the banshee sounds. It was very close, yet quieter than the rumble that just went by. I flashed on my light and realized it was Soona, asleep. In her dreams she was imitating those noises. To her, maybe those were the happy sounds of free spirit dogs, going to and from their hunt, living their lives in packs as nature intended canids to live. For Soona, she was dreaming the good dream. I closed my eyes, let go of all my cares of bad men, and slept the soundless sleep.

When I awoke at six, the sun was illuminating the meadow. The light washed my fears away, and I checked on the dogs. Soona's paw was too sore from her eight days of backpacking in the Beartooths for her to walk the twelve miles. I decided to forego my trip to the glacial cirque, although not without much regret. I knew next year I'd return, but I also knew this meadow wouldn't be the same. There would be no moose, nor spirit dogs howling in the night. The consistent stream of hikers would ensure that. It was only because of the Shoshone dispute, with the land lying fallow, that the animals had reclaimed it. With great reluctance, I packed up and traveled down the dirt road to Fort Washakie. A northern goshawk sat by the side of the road; the cows were still lazing in the gully and Merlin had his day barking and trying to herd them from the truck; a cottontail scurried off the road into the bush; a group of grouse hurried down the hillside; and as I slowly descended the treacherous dirt road, I left Dickinson meadow far behind. Nobody checked for my fishing permit. Nobody really cared. Fall was coming and the snows would be here soon. The wilds would have their way this year at Dickinson Park.

THE WORLD OF FUNGI

For the past two winters, I told Josh I wanted to accompany him on his mushroom trips. This Wednesday we were finally going.

Josh and Kendra owned the best local nursery in town. They were always pushing the horticultural envelope with new and unusual plants, especially ones for zone-denial clients. I was told about their nursery several years ago by a renowned designer and grower in the area, who said I "must get there." On my first trip to his nursery, I met Josh as I went to pay at the cash register. As a landscaper I'm accustomed to receiving discounts at nurseries. The custom is to ask for the discount at the register. So when I asked Josh the question, I was just following the same protocol I used at other local stores.

"Since you're new I'll have to describe our policy to you later."

The next day I received a phone call at home.

"Never, never ask for a discount in front of our customers." It was Josh. He was angry and reprimanding me like a child. Needless to say, that started our relationship off on the wrong foot. But as I couldn't avoid the nursery, I continued to visit, but stayed watchful of his moods. I made an effort to be pleasant, but Josh was always unpredictable.

One memorable moment was when I came in and bought all six of a new variegated *Bilbergia*. When Josh saw them on my cart, he blurted out, "You bought them all?" When I told him I did, he barked, "You bitch!" I was aghast. I went in to pay and told his girlfriend, Kendra, what he'd said. "Oh, he gets so into some of the new merchandise, especially the unusual ones, that he forgets we're in the business of selling."

The talk in the industry was that Josh's moods fluctuated depending on his marijuana use. If you caught him at a good moment, chances are he had toked up not too long before.

After about a year, Josh started to visibly warm up to me. He'd greet me when I came into the nursery, and I was careful to abide by his rules. He even started sending some business my way. I enjoyed him in his good moments. He was extremely knowledgeable about what I love—plants—and was expanding his inventory to include unusual garden art, and strived for excellence in the horticulture arena. One day we struck up a conversation and he told me he was going mushrooming in Oregon.

"We start the season in Oregon, then move to the Mendocino Coast for the winter. As the season wanes there, we go to the Sierras after the snow melts. We gather different mushrooms as the season wears on." He showed me a bag of a few pounds of mushrooms in the back office.

"We're gathering porcinis now. These can fetch several hundred dollars at a restaurant."

I asked him how he got started.

"I took a class at the local community college with one of the greats. He was like the local guru of mushrooms. That was about ten years ago when we first started foraging. In the beginning we were so happy to find just a few of the porcinis or any kind of mushroom we were looking for. Now, we have our spots that we covet. On good days or good seasons, we'll find hundreds."

That was the beginning of my mushroom intrigue. Not that I hadn't gotten close to the fungi world before. Sometimes, when I'd taken horticulture classes at the local arboretum, the Mycological Club met in the adjacent classroom. They were a rowdy bunch: cooking, drinking, eating. Only a narrow, enclosed kitchen separated their meeting room from our classroom. Wonderful aromas wafted into our classroom discussions of *Akebia quinata* and *Parthenocissus*. I'd always sneak a peek into the kitchen where I was offered tastes of earthy smelling dishes and glasses of wine. The mushrooms appeared to be just a minor ingredient— the excuse to cook delectable dishes accompanied by hearty, bawdy discussions.

Every winter over the past two years, I asked Josh about his mushrooming adventures.

"I'd like to come with you sometime."

"Sure, just tell us when."

Kendra, Josh's girlfriend, also mushroomed. Kendra is a delightful, affable, tall, thin, and very athletic blond. Fifteen years younger than Josh, she's his antithesis. Always approachable, she handled all my special-order needs. Her dog Fred, an Australian shepherd mix, hangs at the nursery and is as calm as her.

"This year will be the year I go," I vowed when I saw Josh in September. He was already going up to Oregon during the week for two days at a time. His nursery was doing well, and he and Kendra were taking more and more time off to mushroom. I called Kendra in November.

"Can I go with you when you're up in Mendocino mushrooming?"

"Do you want to go this weekend to Salt Point? The Mycological Society is spending the weekend there. You'd have to camp overnight."

"I can't this weekend. Besides..." I paused. Spending the weekend with a large group of people I didn't know hardly sounded like fun. I was interested in the lore, the experience, what drove Josh to become an aficionado every weekend for months on end. "Besides, I'd rather go with you guys, not so many people."

"Why don't you come up with us to Sea Ranch on the 16th? It's Josh's 50th birthday and we'll be there for a week."

We exchanged numbers and Kendra prepared me with practical suggestions. Bring lots of paper grocery bags and use plastic if it rains; layered clothing, rain gear, and a good knife. I hoped it didn't rain, and realized these guys were serious if they tramped outside for hours rain or shine. We planned that I'd be there for an early start.

Sea Ranch occupies a ten-mile stretch along the wild and beautiful Mendocino coast. Houses are rented out, fully furnished, with the owner setting the price and rules. Unlike many real estate developments, this one is very attractive. The homes are all natural wood and blend among the bishop pines and local chaparral, with the Pacific Ocean raging over rocks in the background. If you are staying at Sea Ranch, you have access to several thousand acres of coastal land and miles of hiking trails. A pass is required on your car and person, and they have their own security guards that do frequent checks. For Josh and Kendra, this was a perfect opportunity to explore unhindered new collecting territory.

Mushroomers seem to be in their own subcategory distinct from other plant enthusiasts. For one thing, most amateur botanists don't collect plants. Either it is illegal, or not environmentally sound, or simply unnecessary. There is no reason to collect plants when you can collect seeds, or take cuttings. The running joke in my zoology classes was that you could always tell a botanist from a zoologist. Botanists are easygoing; zoologists are moody zealots. This rule doesn't seem to apply to mycologists. Now, of course, fungi are technically not plants, so maybe this is the heart of the inconsistency. For starters, they are not even in the same kingdom or classification. Plants are in kingdom Plantae, while fungi are in kingdom Eukarya. Plants make their own food from the sun. Fungi do not photosynthesize, but like humans, eat to live, digesting food outside their bodies through a complicated process using enzymes that break down organic material. Thus, as a life form, they are more like us than plants are.

All this makes for a different breed of collector. Mushroomers are very territorial. Josh explained he and Kendra had their favorite spots and didn't tell anyone about them. They liked to mushroom alone, and had rituals to hide their tracks, like covering the shavings from cleaned mushrooms with fresh dirt so no one would see where they'd been picking. Seeing another collector in your area is always a source of consternation, although of course you act civil and mildly ask, "Where'd you come from?"

We set out soon after I arrived. Kendra had a friend staying with her, a petite woman in her thirties who was in between jobs in San Francisco. Like me, this was her first time and she was only coming along for the ride.

Josh, Kendra, Christine, Fred the dog, and I all piled into the 4x4 and headed north. Josh was looking for some new spots. We turned east off Highway 1 and parked at the bottom of a private road that led to houses on the ridge top. The day was clear and brilliant, a rare winter day along the coast. I was already peeling off layers to leave them in the car when I noticed Josh making a beeline to a large bishop pine by the roadside. Christine and I moved fast to keep up. He was traveling through knee-high coyote brush and blackberries.

"This is it." He pointed to an enormous brown mushroom, about ten inches in diameter.

"That's a beaut! And that's what we're looking for today. Their host tree is bishop pines. You'll find them under the pines. Let's leave that one here and we'll pick it up on the way back. That way we don't have to carry it. I'll show you later how to pick it and clean it. There's a special way to do that before you put it in your pack."

I asked Josh what it was called. "Boletus edulis. Boletes, sometimes known as sweetbreads or Miller's mushroom."

As we moved along the trail, I'd call Josh over and ask about other mushrooms I saw. Usually the response was the same.

"Oh, those are okay to eat. But not as good as the Boletes." And it seems that other mushroomers agree, because that is what everyone was looking for from the first good rains through December. There is even a limit of five pounds per person at Salt Point State Park on Boletes.

A narrow trail guided us through open meadow with brief stands of bishops and Douglas fir. We moved along the trail without seeing much. After about a mile and a half, the terrain still remained dry and rocky. Josh was obviously frustrated with this new site.

"Let's fan out here, and go up the hillside. If we don't find much when we get to the top, let's go to our spot from Sunday."

I was learning fast that mushrooming is a focused, off-trail sport with one's nose to the ground. I hadn't seen any Boletes on my own yet, and really wanted to. I climbed solo up the open meadow, moving between the trees, noting whether they were bishops or Douglas firs. The slope was bone dry and I didn't expect we'd see much. Every so often I glanced around to locate Josh or Kendra. They were down the hill, foraging around in the lower ground. Yet it didn't take long to forget about my companions. I was preoccupied and focused, looking for clues of mushrooms in the duff, watching my step on the steep hillside, while locating bishops and searching under them. When I finally emerged from a tight circle of pines, Kendra, Josh, and Christine were nowhere in sight. I zigzagged down the steep hillside, resting at the trail. I contemplated where they could have gone. I decided to continue farther on the trail since that was where I last saw them. After a quarter mile I came to a large gully of redwoods. Beyond the ravine, the habitat changed, became denser and more wooded. Although I suspected that the mushrooming was better there, when I called, there was no response. If I continued, I'd be wandering too far from the hillside and possibly our group. I decided to retrace my steps back to the car. That had been Josh's plan after all—to return to the car if this place didn't pan out, which I could see it didn't.

It was a good mile or more back to the truck. I knew I wasn't lost—only lost from the group and my thoughts raced to what Josh's response might be. So much of my posture with him was to avoid his unpredictable behavioral responses. Now I was sure he'd be pissed at me. I had, after only a half hour, managed to separate myself from the group, and inconvenience his mushrooming trek. He was being gracious enough to allow me to tag along on his collecting trip, and his birthday weekend, and here I was interrupting the flow. Now instead of mushrooming, I thought they'd have to spend their time searching for me. I began anticipating his agitated and angry response.

On the way to the car, I kept looking for Boletes. By a looming bishop, I spotted what looked like a large brown mushroom. I ducked under some large limbs at the base of the pine. There in the duff was a Bolete. Although I hadn't received the official instruction on how to cut them, it seemed like a simple matter. I knelt down and got out my knife. The mushroom's cap was large, brown, and firm. My knife sliced through the soft white stem, and a primitive feeling overcame me. In my life and work, I've grown and cut many plants. But there was something special and unique about this ritual. Kneeling before this primitive life form in a rite that humans worldwide have shared through the ages. Mushrooms have been sacred throughout human history. *Food of the Gods*, *Plant of Immortality*, I was falling into a deep cultural memory. I cut the stem and gently scrubbed off the excess dirt with my knife. Carefully, instinctively, like I was gathering a holy object, I placed the Bolete in a paper bag and into my pack.

As I stood up, for a moment the magic held. Then, in a flash, I returned to my present dilemma. I was still thinking about Josh being pissed. "At least I found one while separated from the group," I rationalized.

No one had made it back to the truck. I took off my coat and dumped it in the truck bed. It was getting hot. I decided to double back. That way I could catch them on their return. They were probably just a few steps behind me, I thought, yet I was relieved they weren't waiting for me.

I took the high trail back and crossed the first small ravine that separated the car from the hill we'd been last climbing on together. I looked up and saw Josh walking down from an even higher trail.

"Where is everybody?" He was carrying a bag full of mushrooms and had obviously lost track of time while foraging, just like I had.

Funny. Looks like Josh was lost too. In fact, now that we'd met up, it was the others that were missing. All my mental gyrations became comical, and totally unnecessary. I was worried about nothing. In fact, the whole episode just had me looking in the mirror.

"I'm pissed at Kendra. I told her to go up the hill and then double back. Let's go back to the car where I left my walkie-talkie and put some new batteries in it. Then we'll try and find them."

We walked back to the truck and I showed Josh my Boletus. "Nice. I didn't find much here. This spot's too dry. We'll find Kendra and continue further up the coast. First I'm gonna go find that mushroom we saw around here." I was amused. Josh couldn't be that annoyed at our lost friends. He and I took about fifteen minutes locating that initial mushroom. For some reason, we both kept getting turned around in the circle of pines and blackberry brambles. Finally, I came across it. We bagged it then hopped in the truck, rendezvousing with Kendra and Christine about two miles up. They had continued beyond the redwood gully I had seen, instead of going up the hill. In doing so, they had clearly out-mushroomed both Josh and me. They approached the truck with two full bags of prize Boletes.

We spent the next several hours in prime Boletus country. Huckleberries growing under the bishops indicated the presence of more groundwater. We all came out with bags and bags of mushrooms. And I learned a few more lessons. The first was about the Spy. The Spy is a mushroom that is small and white. Although edible, no one collects Spies. Spies are the indicator for Boletes, the true prize. Where you see Spies, there are sure to be Boletes nearby, and for some reason, the Spy was a lot easier for me to find than the Boletes, maybe because they're white instead of tan. I found most of my best mushrooms using Spies, also known as *Clitophilus prunulus*.

My second lesson was about myself. I started to notice that, although Josh was in a fine mood, I was guarded around him, alert for his unpredictability. I was striving to keep him happy, stay upbeat, and be a good student. The ridiculousness of my situation, all the effort I was expending on this, made me realize that I had no idea what would set him off. The absurdity of my response hit me. I couldn't modulate his moods by my responses, nor should I even have to. I only could be responsible for my response to his moodiness. At this revelation, I gave up and enjoyed being with the group and finding mushrooms.

Mushrooming is actually hard work. It's all off-trail, sometimes through thick brush and it requires focused attention to the details of textures of leaf and litter.

"You'll be good at this," Kendra said to me. "You're used to looking at and differentiating textures and colors of plant material."

By noon I was starving. I had two full shopping bags of Boletes plus my backpack was full. I didn't have room to carry any more. We headed back to the car. On the way, I met up with Kendra and pointed out some Spies.

"I'm getting the hang of this Spy thing. It really helped me find mushrooms."

"This here is a prime spot." We were standing on the north side of a large ravine bordered by bishops and redwoods. "On Sunday we picked so many Boletes here. But there's been other people here since. Sometimes when we find a good spot, we remove the Spies along with the Boletes. That way no one will know it's a primo place."

Wow, this was a competitive sport.

Back at their rental, Kendra was relaxing with Christine on the porch, while Josh was laying Boletes from the previous days' forages out onto the kitchen counter. I was making notes at the kitchen table, trying to remember all the Latin names of the mushrooms we saw in the morning.

Within a few minutes, Josh had gone downstairs and returned with a very large dehydrator, full of mushrooms. He sat on the floor and began bagging the dried edibles.

"This layer here is just the gills. Restaurateurs covet this part. Put it in soups or dishes, and it flavors anything up perfectly." Josh used to work as a chef in restaurants. He had the know-how and the connections.

"This bag is worth about $40. We don't do this for the money anyways. We're happy if it can just pay for our expenses."

I told him how surprised I was. I had thought his mushrooming was a side business, because he and Kendra brought so much intensity to it.

"Nah. We do things like take our entire staff and their spouses out to dinner for trade. Last month we had sixteen people at Indigo's in the city, all in credit, and we still had money left over. We can walk into any Japanese restaurant with Matsutakes and get a meal on the spot. I do some sales out of the store in the back. Sometimes the staff gets annoyed. But it's not that much. Besides, this year the market's been flooded and the profit margins are way down. Too many people mushrooming."

I asked him if there were more mushroom collectors now than when he first started.

"You bet. There are over 300 people in the Mycological Society of San Francisco alone."

"Why are people getting so into it all of a sudden?"

"Well, it's because people like me take people like you out for fun, and then you get into it more and more. I really shouldn't be sharing all my spots and knowledge so easily, but I don't mind because it's kind of fun to introduce my friends to it."

Somehow, I doubted that was the real reason for the sudden rise in foraging. Probably it had more to do with people's culinary taste and restaurants buying from hobbyists. I know in my own business, plants go through fads, fading in and out of fashion. I assumed the mycological world was no exception.

He finished emptying the dehydrator and stacked it all up on the table. Josh opened the fridge and pulled out more bags of Boletes from previous days' forages. In fact, when I opened the refrigerator looking for a drink, I hardly saw any food. The fridge was stuffed with paper bags full of Boletes.

"Kendra! You've got to come in and help clean these for drying. We can't just leave them." I could hear escalating agitation in Josh's voice. But Kendra didn't budge. She had told me earlier that I was the first landscaper to know she was pregnant. Now she was taking a well-earned rest.

"Forget it, Josh. I don't want to do it now." She was firm, yet still easygoing with him.

"I'll help you," I said. I realized I was going home with bags of Boletes and had no idea how to prepare them. Josh showed me how to cut the Boletes for drying.

"The cap and gills are the best. The stem's okay to eat too but not as good. Slice the cap really thin, fry it in some olive oil with salt, and that's good eatin'."

There were mounds of Boletes and pretty soon I was working alone.

"Kendra, you really must get in here! We can't let all these mushrooms go bad." Josh's stress was mounting, demanding, imploring her to start work. Kendra remained calm, unruffled. She continued her conversation on the porch with Christine. Josh retreated to the phone and began wheeling and dealing fresh and dried mushrooms with restaurateurs.

I finished cleaning and preparing the mushrooms. Finally, Kendra and Christine emerged from the porch and Josh got off the phone. Josh was more irritable than ever, criticizing Kendra again about the mushrooms that needed to be dried.

"It's your job too, Kendra. That was your responsibility to bag them all and load up the dryer."

I watched her. She was brilliant in her response, like watching an experienced judo artist outmaneuver the common criminal. Her easygoing nature was unperturbed by his increasing craziness. She addressed his concerns but was firm with his moods. I was learning from an expert.

"I'm going to make lunch now, Josh. That will just have to wait till later."

With that, Josh made another phone call. When he hung up, he informed us he was going off for firewood to a neighbor's house and left in the truck. After an hour when he hadn't returned, it was clear that he also was taking care of himself by acquiring some dope. Josh was happy. Kendra was happy and she hadn't allowed him to dump on her nor had she taken on his discontent.

Josh returned and we all had lunch together. I said my goodbyes, loaded my Boletes in the car, and headed for home. As I drove home, I was happy too. It had been a good morning. I'd learned some new lessons about plants and about myself, along with cementing new friendships. The fog rolled in like a thick layer of cotton batting. The drive home along the coast highway would be slow and breathtaking.

WILD CATS

Looking for Lynx in Northwest Wyoming

I t was a beautiful, cloudless morning when I pulled on my snowshoes. The crisp chill in the winter air only meant I'd slowly be stripping off layers of clothing for the steep hike through a series of layered limestone reefs. The access road, which is my trail, hugs hanging flanks of ancient seabed cliffs. There are two reefs and my destination is the uppermost. The road switchbacks west along the second reef, traversing over glacial pavement. A maze of old logging roads carve farther into the rocky cliffs above. Spring through fall, this is a wet place, as hidden springs run underground, emerging through the cracks in the limestone.

A friend who'd hunted here last fall said he'd seen so many snowshoe hare tracks they were like scribbles in the snow. Winter visitors head farther north to recreate, and as this road has a locked gate at the entrance, I'm assured of a quiet respite.

A recent snowstorm left soft, deep snow and it's a heart workout in my snowshoes. The forest is thick on both sides until a sharp turn signals a second locked gate to a telephone service road. I know after I pass this bend the climb steepens, one side against the blocky wall with a vertical drop on the other side. The second reef was supposedly where the hares are clustered. I'm heading there until I see the road is blocked farther ahead by an avalanche of snow at its most narrow juncture. I decide to explore the first reef that lies beyond the telephone access road, but while snowshoeing back down to the gate, I'm hit with an explosion of snowshoe hare tracks.

Snowshoe hare tracks are exciting because they are so big, and testify to how well adapted these animals are to snow-covered habitat. Their oversized hind feet are generously covered with fur, and where I'm sinking, they are having a party in the snow. What's interesting to me is not just these tracks, but their feeding evidence. This mountain has experienced a lot of logging as well as fire activity, resulting in numerous copses of young spruce. The evidence indicates the hares are standing on their feet, chewing off the lower tips of spruce branches. Nipped twigs and gnawed-off branches are strewn everywhere underneath these groves.

Several summers ago, I saw a woman juggling armloads of equipment walking to the nearby forest. We chatted for a while and I asked what she was doing. She told me she was an independent contractor for the Forest Service. "I'm working on a vegetation study."

The Forest Service, she said, was using her information to understand if this was good lynx habitat. I knew the Shoshone Forest Service was working on their twenty-year management plan, a massive undertaking that revisits guidelines for a range of issues, including timber, grazing, oil and gas, and wildlife. I asked her how her work was helping the Forest Service determine the management approach for lynx; what was the connection between our local vegetation and the meat-eating lynx? The connection, it turns out, is the hare—that speedy animal that lynx prey on.

Lynx, being listed under the Endangered Species Act as a threatened species, needed proper consideration and protection in the Forest Service's plan. I wasn't exactly clear how tying flagging of various colors to trees, then using her survey equipment, equated with analyzing good habitat. But that conversation piqued my interest in lynx. Thus, my underlying reason for a hard snowshoe up the reefs—are there any lynx preying on these hares?

I'd seen snowshoe hares in spring where this contractor was surveying, as well as other locations farther up the wide basin where I live, which are only accessible by snowmobile in winter. The contractor told me her plan was to survey there as well and her concern was grizzlies. There are a lot of bears in the upper reaches of the drainages where she'd be camping solo for several days. I told her I'd pay a visit to check on her.

We also have white-tailed jackrabbits, and their tracks are very similar in size to snowshoe hares, therefore easily confused. After a few hours of exploring for tracks along the reefs, the only other spoor I saw came from coyotes. With the increase of access roads and snowmobile trails, coyotes have an easier time venturing farther into deep snow areas of the winter backcountry where snowshoe hares live. The evidence is mixed on whether coyotes are competing with lynx for food by reducing the snowshoe hare population. Fewer snowshoe hares, fewer lynx.

Lynx are made for snow with their huge paws. In winter, snowshoe hares are 96% of their diet. But lynx in their southernmost ranges, like in Washington, Idaho, and Montana, are in trouble. Climate change is the main reason. Warming temperatures reduce snow cover. In particular, soft deep snow gives lynx the competitive advantage over other animals. Increasing numbers of forest fires destroy snowshoe hare habitat. Researchers and conservationists are stuck as bystanders just watching the decline of lynx numbers throughout the West.

The Yellowstone region is at the southern tip of lynx historic range, which made them uncommon historically in the park. But there have been several sightings in the last fifteen years, mostly through confirmed tracks. A set of tracks was verified in 2014 near the northeast entrance, just a skip and jump over the mountains from these reefs. In fact, looking on the park's website, they have a map with some red dots indicating confirmed DNA lynx evidence. There are only two measly dots in my valley that were documented sightings during a twelve-year period between 1996 and 2008.

Sapling forests from regeneration such as burns or old logging are good hare habitat providing excellent cover and food. Because our volcanic soils drain quickly and are nutrient poor, forest understory cover here is limited. Some exceptions might be the granitic Wind Rivers or Togwotee Pass in the Bridger-Tetons. According to Kerry Murphy, biologist for the Shoshone Forest Service, snowshoe hare studies in my area found only pockets of hare activity, not enough to support lynx. It takes a lot of hares to support a lynx population. Several extensive lynx studies were completed in the Beartooths and Yellowstone area in the last twenty years. Biologists found that during flush snowshoe hare years in Montana, a few lynx would venture south in search of new territory, only to eventually leave due to poor prey populations. The same situation occurred when lynx were reintroduced into the Colorado Rockies during the early 2000s. Some dispersed north and took up residency in the Wind Rivers and Bridger-Teton range, but after a year most, if not all, left for happier hunting grounds.

Truthfully, I wasn't sure if I could tell a lynx from a large bobcat. Anecdotally, I'd also heard that our previous mail lady, who lived here most of her life (which immediately qualified her, in the mind of the local gossip machine, to be able to discriminate between a lynx and a bobcat), had seen a lynx at my mailbox. Maybe a case of mistaken identity, but maybe not.

Those nipped buds and twigs—evidence of snowshoe hare in dense yet young spruce/fir forest—educated me about potential lynx habitat. Ten miles up my dirt road, heading west just a few miles from the Yellowstone Park boundary line, there is similar habitat that also experienced burns and logging in the 1940s and 1950s. The following spring, I looked around and sure enough, lots of snowshoe hare evidence there as well. So we definitely have hares, but do we have lynx, besides just two red dots on a page?

Hare populations, like other rabbit populations, run in cycles. I asked Dr. Charles Preston at the Draper Museum what caused these cycles. He joked that if he could figure that out, he'd die happy. These boom-and-bust cycles regulate the rabbit populations, and with it the bobcat and lynx as well. Yet nature always throws a wrench into the works, and I'd read that in some southernmost hare populations, like possibly the area around Yellowstone, these cycles don't occur, but instead the hares remain stable at low densities. Maybe this might also explain the persistently low population of lynx around here.

Even with all my exploring, lynx tracks weren't forthcoming. Yet I did begin to consider the three cats that live here, their interactions, and what kinds of cat fights might ensue. Lynx and bobcat obviously share similar food preferences. Panthera's big cat scientist Dr. Mark Elbroch says that makes it difficult for them to share similar habitat.

"Where they share range, lynx typically stick to the higher elevations, where deeper snows give them the competitive advantage, and bobcats take control of the lowlands, where they assume the dominant role and exclude lynx through aggressive interactions."

Lynx and bobcat can occasionally hybridize. In a study in Michigan in 2004, DNA evidence revealed three out of twenty individuals tested were hybrids of lynx and bobcat—blynx. Who knows if this is happening in lynx range around Yellowstone, where a rare species may come into contact with a more common species? Doing a study in the Yellowstone region might be quite revealing. If blynx are capable of reproducing, we may just have to be satisfied with hybrid lynx in the Yellowstone ecosystem.

Cats in a Timeless Maze

Comb Ridge rises dramatically in the Utah desert skyline, an impressive eighty-mile north-south sandstone geologic fold. A walk up from its eastern incline leads to a steep, formidable drop-off on its western edge. Only a mile wide, the eastern approach contains deep canyons harboring ancient dwellings. These prehistoric homes lie under overhangs, fill canyon recesses, and are stuffed into cliff niches. Sometimes a sheer vertical wall, punctuated with alcoves of stone houses, makes plain the only access must have been rope ladders, long vanished with the desert elements. A hike into these canyon ruins reveals thousand-year-old dried-up corn cobs, impressions in boulders used as metates carved out of hundreds of hours of hand labor, pottery shards, and walls spattered with clay-red handprints where women once ground corn into meal. Locals tell of an ancient highway that connected Comb Ridge to Chaco Canyon, two hundred miles away. There are stories of footholds etched into the western cliffs, enabling athletic Puebloans to climb the ridge, and complete their journey on the road to the sacred lands beyond.

I've been drawn to this landscape for years, an area President Obama designated as Bears Ears National Monument. One of the largest canyons in the Comb Ridge complex is Mule Canyon, a wide valley wash surrounded by sheer sandstone cliffs. The canyon is a sunny, easy hike, and its few ruins are hard to spot since they hang high up the canyon walls. I was following a bobcat, his prints easily visible along the sandy canyon bottom. He was on a direct route, according to his tracks, probably returning from a nightly hunt. The tracks engrossed me for over a mile, when suddenly they veered off to the right, into a narrow steep ravine. As I changed course to follow them, I looked up, and high up the steep canyon walls I noticed alcoves filled with man-made walls dividing a series of rooms. This large habitation, unoccupied since the 12th century, accessible only with ropes or ladders, was probably quickly abandoned, possibly due to warfare and drought. It was within this masonry that my bobcat disappeared. This shadowy predator had taken up residence in what I imagined to be a perfect home for one of the few animals that could navigate these ledges—the bobcat could now use them well to his advantage as protection from his human enemies.

Access to the ruins was through a narrow side wash. I circled the dense brush along sandy bottoms for a better vantage point. As I stood at the cliff base looking up, there was my bobcat. I found it ironic that he was living in a man-made housing development that even I could not access. After considering my presence for a few moments, he must have decided I was uninteresting and vanished into the deep recesses of the alcoves.

My sighting left me thinking about who or what was using the thousands of ruins throughout the region. There was some poetic justice in humans building houses now used as wildlife retreats, where animals could hide from humans who hunt and trap them. Bobcat trapping was at an all-time high due to pelt prices, driven by demand in China and Russia. Pelts could be worth upwards of $800 each. This bobcat was probably too far afield for a trapper who is required by law to regularly check his traps, but not for a hunter with dogs. Yet here he was, safe in an abandoned housing development.

Encountering that bobcat reminded me of another story of a cat living amongst ruins in the Southwest. In 1934, Frank C. Hibben was given a grant from the Southwestern Conservation League to spend a year studying mountain lions in Arizona and New Mexico. As the field naturalist, Hibben had only one way to find lions: by accompanying professional lion hunters doing controls for state game agencies and the Biological Survey. Hibben tells a tale of riding with houndsman Giles Goswick deep into the canyons of Arizona tracking a cattle-killing cougar. Interestingly, Hibben says that of thirty-two reports of cougar-killed cattle by ranchers he investigated, thirty were false claims.

The cougar they followed that day was a skilled stealth artist who coursed narrow ledges along gulches with steep overhanging cliffs, perplexing the dogs who kept losing track of the animal. Shadowing their lead dog through a narrow ravine, Hibben and Giles scrambled over centuries-old fallen trees and canyon pools, with the barking of dogs echoing down the canyon. As the canyon walls grew steeper, the chasm dimmer, and the mysterious noises along with the din of barking echoed louder, the little gulch grew eerier.

Giles stayed ahead, concentrating on trying to find a lion track in the patches of sand on the canyon floor. Suddenly Hibben shouted to Giles, "Look up there—to the left. Up there in that shadow," pointing and waving his hand. Giles undoubtedly thought Hibben had seen the lion on an overhang, but instead he found, shaded by the overhanging cliff, two caves, one above the other, with fragments of man-made adobe masonry and mortar housing a window cut-out.

Even with all the excitement of their lion chase, the dogs still howling in the distance, the men stopped to examine this ancient ruin. They surmounted a low ledge and stood at the lower cave entrance. Fragments of walls and partitions still clung to the cave floor. Fingerprints of the long-dead builders were outlined in the mortar where they had pressed it hard between the stones. The usual pack rat occupants were making the cave their home, but perched on top of the rat's stick and cacti mounds was a yucca sandal with the ties and strings still intact. There was even a visible hole in the heel of the sandal.

The second cave fifty feet above, not big enough for human habitation, was the showstopper. As their eyes became accustomed to the darkened environment, they spotted sticks protruding outward in all directions from the cave's arched opening. The twigs were bound with blue and yellow colored bands, with feathers on the ends.

"Giles! They're arrows," Hibben exclaimed, while Giles was already pulling out his lariat rope that he carried around his waist. Deftly, Giles threw his rope, barely reaching the lowermost of the protruding shafts, and three arrows fell at the men's feet. The arrows were preserved perfectly by the dry climate—wooden arrows fitted with three feathers and a notch for the bow string. Maybe two or three hundred of these arrows protruded from the small opening above.

Caught in a timeless moment, the men forgot where they were or why they were there. The barking of the dogs brought them back. The cougar that had led them to this place had been forgotten momentarily. Carefully, they placed the arrows and the sandal on a ledge in the lower cave, to remain in situ, and as they looked up, they saw the dogs had treed their victim, who was hanging from a gnarled spruce limb at the end of the canyon.

Hibben ends his story by writing: "The long-deserted cliff house in the narrow canyon with the ceremonial arrow cave above it created an atmosphere of antiquity which was not ordinary background for any cougar. Perhaps this lion was the reincarnation of one of the old cliff dwellers prowling the tumbled masonry and the dark caves of his forefathers."

After his year riding with government-hired houndsmen, Hibben wrote a detailed paper in the University of New Mexico Bulletin on all aspects of mountain lions. In it, he advocates for lions to be reclassified as trophy game animals instead of a bounty predator, something that would not happen for over thirty years. Maybe a whisper from the ancient cliff dwellers led him to a change of heart for some protections for a cat that has been on this continent longer than humans.

Following a Cougar to a Kill

I found a pile of freshly collected dirt and pine needles under a large fir. It had the obvious signs of the only animals around here that cover their scat—felines. I pushed aside the dirt and found cougar scat, so fresh and meaty looking that it was obvious this cat had just killed and eaten. Cougar biologist Toni Ruth describes a typical lion-kill scene: The cougar will drag his kill usually under a tree, then cover it, which aides in hiding the smell to keep scavengers away and helps keep it fresh. A deer can take several days to consume. The cat eats, sleeps, and sets up a latrine nearby. Sometimes cougars will just eat the organs and leave. They need the nutritious organs since they lost the ability somewhere in evolutionary time to convert carotenoids like beta carotene into vitamin A.

I'd been following cougar tracks and scrapes, and looking for kills for years. I'd found many old kill signs, but only once before did I find a fresh kill. It was spring, and I'd begun a day hike as dusk was approaching. I parked on a dirt side road, then walked a valley I knew led to a viewpoint at the ridgeline saddle. Tight stands of sagebrush lie at the bottom of this small drainage. The sagebrush slides seamlessly into stands of short pines and firs, cut by culverts fed by ephemeral streams in early spring. In the past I'd found old cougar kills within this forest. Within a few miles, the forest opens to wide meadows as you approach the pass. It was here that my dog beelined for a large fir beside the creek. I followed and found a freshly killed dead deer covered with sticks and duff. I knew that cougar had to be around somewhere, watching me. I spent a little time exploring, looking for his tracks in the receding snow, but a thunderstorm came barreling in. I took cover under a copse of trees, hid there for a while, but soon I was drenched and the sky was pounding with thunder claps and lightning. I also remembered the road I'd taken floods easily, turning into gumbo, making it impassable. If I didn't hurry down the mountain, I'd be stuck. So I couldn't return to put a camera on that kill.

Today, I thought, if I could locate the kill, I was close to home and I had one trail camera I could use. Since this scat was obviously extremely fresh, I began hunting in an ever-widening circle looking for the kill site. Yet I found nothing. I walked into the nearby forest where a light wet snow still covered the ground from the previous evening. It was there I found the cat's prints. I backtracked the cougar, who had crossed through several properties, until I easily found his kill, a young buck. He'd made the kill almost directly behind an absentee owner's home. The deer use their yard all winter so that was no surprise. The carcass had been dragged within a stand of tight willows surrounded by trees. Snow was melting and the area was soggy. The cat had started on his kill already, entering through the rib cage which is typical, and eaten the organs. I returned with my trail camera and placed it at the kill site.

I called one neighbor who owns a large horse ranch to alert them of the kill in the neighborhood. They always have a few new foals, so this way she could keep a watch on them. She told me there was a young grizzly scouting their hay fields not far from this cat's hidden carcass. It got me wondering if the bear would bounce the cougar off his kill. Cougars are subordinate predators, and bears kick them off their kills 50% of the time. A bear can smell a carcass up to twenty miles away. I was betting on the bear.

But I had other questions. First, this cougar seemed to be acting somewhat like cougars that live in urban-wild-land settings, and where I live is not that. The majority of this landscape is public lands with a handful of large ranches, and very few homes, most of which are vacant during winter. Yet this cat's latrine was one-quarter of a mile away, and not used repeatedly. That meant it was coming and going to its kill, returning only under cover of darkness. We have few residents here in the winter, our dirt road is lightly used, and if today had been any other blustery spring weekend, I believe this cat would have act-ed differently. But this happened to be Memorial Day, and some of the nearby vacation homes were occupied, and people from towns in the surrounding areas were coming for overnight camping. And while this particular prop-erty was owned by out-of-staters, the owners picked this weekend to visit. I alerted them to the kill site, and told them to carry bear spray just in case that bear decided to make a meal of the cat's deer.

If the bear hadn't been hanging around, I could have set up a blind, watching the cougar return. But instead I relied on my camera, checking it daily. I even wondered with the increased Memorial Day road traffic and occupied cabins if the cougar would return. After all, he finished the internal organ meat already.

Over the course of the next several nights, my cougar did return three times to feed. My first visitor came at 3:45 a.m., a coyote. The coyote fed for fifteen minutes, skittish the whole time, then left. Within twenty-five minutes after the coyote disappeared, the cougar arrived and fed for forty minutes. With the coyote feeding for such a short time, I'm betting he sensed the cougar was in the vicinity, giving reason for the him to high-tail out of there.

Magpies along with the coyote visited during the day. A fox arrived under cover of darkness when both the cougar and coyote were gone. Yet the bear never showed up. He moved down the valley, apparently more interested in grass and grains to clear out his system than meat during this time of year.

Because cougars cover their kills, it is rare to stumble upon one. Wolves kill in open country and wolf-killed carcasses are easy to spot. Look for bird activity, particularly ravens and golden eagles circling above or intense activity flying back and forth. Birds will lead you to kill sites. But cougars intentionally try not to attract predacious birds and other predators by stashing their kills under brush or trees, then covering them with dirt or snow. I've done a lot of cougar tracking, but since cougars kill infrequently, tracks don't usually lead you to their kills.

The first kill I found didn't qualify as using any skills on my part. I simply followed my dog's nose. But this find had relied on my knowledge of cougar behavior. It included recognizing and subsequently investigating a covered pile of scat under the umbrella of a large fir. Finding fresh scat doesn't usually indicate a kill, but I recognized a fresh meat scat of a cougar, which tipped me off to a nearby kill.

Recalling that cougars set up latrines within an area of their kill site, I walked in ever enlarging circles, looking for the latrine. Theoretically, this should have worked, as I've done that before at old kill sites. Yet since this was close to residences, it took scouting for tracks, then backtracking the cat. I felt like I'd taken Cougar Class 101 and passed the final exam.

Several weeks later I was off to check a trail camera. I walked up a small rise, then paused to look across a wide open meadow surrounded by forest. At that moment, a figure emerged from the trees into the open. In a split-second, I realized I was watching a cougar, relaxed in his baseline gait, coursing through the grass. For some reason, he didn't see or catch my scent until he was halfway across the expanse, directly in front of me about 125 feet downhill. Just like a cat, he hid behind the sole tree midway, then moments later in three bounds he was within the cover of the forest. After years of tracking, this was the first cougar I'd ever seen, and it was a delicious and long sighting. With good snow still on the ground, his prints revealed he was a male, and probably the male that killed the deer by my house. I backtracked him to a scrape under some trees, then front-tracked him to a place I know well, a steep slope leading to an area I call the basement.

Cougars are exciting because they are so elusive. Tracking them, finding their scrapes, their day beds, and maybe even glimpsing one, is like discovering a secret codex. You spend years decoding a treasure map. You follow the map, but the map only leads you on a journey that reveals hidden riches within the journey itself.

THE POND

In 2019 I vowed to take my old dog, Koda, to a nearby hidden pond every day for a swim. Koda had elbow dysplasia. He also developed laryngeal paralysis, a debilitating neurological disease that affects the vagus nerve, slowly paralyzing and compressing the larynx opening, making it harder and harder to breathe. The "fix" is a "tie back" where one side of the cartilage is pulled back to open the air passage. But it's crude medicine, as it's certain the dog will at some point aspirate, filling his lungs and requiring an emergency visit to the vet. Since Koda would also not be able to swim with the procedure, I settled on doing nothing but his favorite exercise. The heartbreaking disease usually ends with the dog's back legs giving out, probably due to lack of oxygen supply. Swimming made Koda happy and kept his legs strong.

I set up a self-challenge to see if I could go every day to the pond. It's only a ten-minute drive. The pond is directly off a main highway, but a steep, downhill, broken two-track makes it almost inaccessible as well as hidden. It's also a corridor for wildlife, particularly grizzly bears. Cattle grazing on open range find the pond in late August, mucking up the meadow and leaving their filth along the edges. One previous summer a bull decided to make it his home for the entire summer season. The pond was soon unpleasant.

But for some unknown reason, Koda's last year of life, the cows kept away. Without their insistent grazing, plants I'd never seen in previous years erupted in color and shrubs fruited.

The steep grade alongside the forest evens out, opening into a large meadow. The pond has no inlet or outlet, but is fed by snowmelt from an underground stream off the massive limestone cliffs above the highway. The concealed lake outlet emerges in a ravine that descends over 700 feet into the canyon below. An animal trail is the only access through a steep defile, where the gorge widens and the river slows. A mile downstream, the canyon walls close in and the river becomes a raging torrent.

Over the last several years, record snowfall has grown the pond into a real lake. Surrounded on the majority of its circumference by spruce and Douglas fir, the expanding lake consumed tree trunks. Over many years, I'd bring my dog for a swim. I knew the best rocks to sun or stand on, and for the best vantage to throw the dummy for the dog to retrieve. Over the last few years, my rock edged farther and farther into the lake.

During this last year of Koda's life, I gave him a good time every day at the pond. Because I went daily, I decided to chronicle my observations and changes in the pond life.

Life at the Pond

Early April – I parked at the road, and we trudged down through thick wet snow to the pond's edge. A layer of thick ice lay on top—still frozen. A single set of wolf tracks ran across the lake. An old snowmobile track crossed the ice. The snow made it easy to find recent coyote and moose tracks.

April 23 – The ice is thinning. It's broken up enough near the shore for a cold swim for Koda. He doesn't mind the freezing water. In fact, he likes to roll in the snow after a swim to help dry off.

May 5 – The two-track is still too muddy to drive down. I don't want to ruin the road any further, so we walked the road from the highway. Big grizzly tracks were by the lake. The bears are waking up.

May 9 – A photographer friend tells me he calls this Ruddy Duck Lake. Today I heard a lot of Wilson's snipe calls. I never have seen a snipe, but I hear their calls frequently in spring. What I'm actually hearing is the wing whirl of their outspread tail feathers as the birds are in flight. It's a winnowing sound that descends hauntingly. The forest is alive with their *hu-hu-hu* during spring when the males are defending their territory and attracting mates. For a long time, I confused the sound with that of an owl.

May 15 – I'm not a duck person, but I'm learning as spring arrives and the pond fills with ducks. I bring a bird book with me and binoculars. The ducks want nothing to do with a swimming dog. There are a lot of ruddy ducks, golden eye pairs, ring-neck pairs, and grebes. Yellow-rumped warblers are numerous, catching bugs. They are very proficient at it. They sit on a nearby tree, then quickly swoop in and catch insects mid-air. Today is our first warm day and we are having a large hatch of bugs. Baby boreal toads are plentiful along the lakeshore. The dirt road was completely dry and drivable.

May 16 – The bugs are hatching, but with a slight wind it's bearable by the shoreline. Spring beauty flowers, *Claytonia lanceolata*, cover the marshy areas. The leaves and flowers are a nice snack. I think they are one of the tastiest wild plants in the ecosystem. Today the wind is westerly, forcing the dummy quickly toward the opposite side of the lake. It moved faster than Koda could reach it, and he gave up and came back to shore. We watched it slowly cross the entire lake.

Koda and I walked through the spruce forest to retrieve it. The blowdowns and beetle kill are thick in the woods. Poor Koda had a really hard time negotiating all the downed tree barriers. We retrieved the dummy and circumambulated the lake. There is another smaller lake just beyond. This area is wet and marshy, and with a granitic basement, the plateau holds the snowmelt runoff for much of the year.

May 17 – We arrived late in the day as I had a plan. Elk were grazing on the other side of the pond when we arrived. After Koda's swim, I spent an hour at dusk driving up and down the highway glassing and calling for great gray owls. They would be nesting now. Great grays don't build nests, but use nests of other birds. Around here, that usually means red-tailed hawk nest sites. There used to be several good nest sites, but since the Forest Service logged the area, those sites are gone. But as I was driving home in the darkness, a large bird flew across the road.

May 19 – Canada geese have arrived at the pond. It's super cold today. Hundreds of swallows are dancing and skimming the water catching bugs. I noticed the spring beauties close up in the cold, but new ones are still emerging. Grizzlies enjoy *Claytonias*, but from my observations they are able to sniff them out while still dormant. That way all the nutrition still lies in the bulbs. Haven't seen a track lately.

May 24 – Green-winged teal are dabbling around the pond edges; Canada geese emerge with five tiny yellow goslings. Ruddy duck with eleven ducklings. The male ruddys are very unusual with their sky-blue bills. Ring-necked ducks; and mallards have shown up; common golden eye; eared grebes. After Koda's swim, I drove across the road and left him in the car. He can't hike the steep climb to the cliffs that feed the lake anymore. I explore this area every spring to look for orchids. Fairyslippers, *Calypso bulbosa*, are common, but sometimes I find mountain lady slippers or glacier lilies. The trail is through thick forest with a maze of downed timber. If the Back Country Horsemen, a group that helps the Forest Service clear trails, have scheduled it for clearing this year, then the trail is passable. But they cleared it last year, and already new blowdowns have obstructed passage in spots. As the trail climbs to the plateau above, visibility around corners is slim and without the dog, I have only my own senses to cue me to bears. I watch for bear sign, but that's not always a reliable tell. Every so often I yell, "Hey bear!" This is one of the grizzly corridors that leads to the lake below. I usually see bear sign in the spring, and sure enough, there's a nice print, along with a smaller one—a grizzly mom and her cub have passed through. As I round a curve, an animal slowly waddles down the trail out of sight. It's a porcupine, a very unusual sighting these days. Porcupines used to be plentiful in the higher elevation, but they've all but vanished for years. Studies have been conducted throughout the Mountain West with no answers.

June 3 – 5:30 p.m. A surprise when a hunter emerged from the trees since few people know of this place. We chatted and he told me he was hunting black bears. Wyoming has a spring and fall black bear season, but in grizzly bear territory, no baiting is allowed. Outside of the grizzly zone, bait stands are allowed and hunters compete for tags for bait areas. Frankly, I don't see how baiting is fair chase, and why anyone wants to kill a bear anyways. Bears are incredibly intelligent. Grizzly bears have been compared to the great apes in their intelligence. At least Wyoming doesn't allow dogs to run bears like some states do. We have a lot of black bears in our area. I know this because I catch dozens on my trail cameras all summer long. Our hunt quotas never fill and that is probably because hunting black bears without baiting is difficult. Because we have grizzlies here, black bears keep a fairly low profile. They know when grizzlies are in the area and keep their distance. This hunter said he saw a bear on the other side of the river, but it was too far away to shoot. He had hiked down the ravine via the animal trail, spying the bear on the other bank. I wondered how he might have even retrieved the bear if he'd shot it. There's no road access and he'd have to cross the river in high water, then recross again but carrying the bear.

June 14 – Early morning at the pond. Koda is anxious to swim. It's overcast, dark, and looks like rain is moving in. There are very few ducks. The geese and goslings have made a mess all over the rock I like to stand on. The ruddy ducklings are practicing swimming.

June 15 – A surprise awaited me when I arrived. A couple in a truck with two dogs were camped at the lakeside. They had a soft camper shell, which folded and pulled out to the side of the truck, creating a tent-like structure. An interesting setup. The young couple was from Las Vegas. The fellow is in the Reserves working as an airline mechanic and she's a nurse. They told me they were interested in moving to the Greater Yellowstone area. I asked how they heard about the pond since there are no signs and the dirt two-track, which is a Forest Service road, has no marker on the highway. They said the Cooke City Visitor's Center gave them a map of off-road pull-out campsites. To me it sounded like a ludicrous suggestion since this area is a pinch-point corridor for grizzly bears—not the best camping spot for tourists.

June 21 – 8:30 a.m. The accumulation of old and fresh geese droppings on the stone granite slab is now overwhelming. I can't stand there anymore and am forced to use the muddy lakeshore, which the geese also have mucked up. All their goslings were hanging around the slab when I arrived. The geese have taken over.

The winds have changed during the last few months since the floater dummy went to the opposite shore. That was east to west winds. Now the winds are facing us consistently for the last several weeks, west to east. This breeze is much better for Koda because I can throw the dummy farther out, but then it will return in our direction.

The lake is rising. There has been sufficient snow this year, though not like the last two years. The cliffs and its reefs feed into this pond through an underground aquifer that filled during the last several years of record snows. I can tell it is rising relative to my sitting rock from last year. Last year's sitting rock is now about thirty feet beyond the shoreline into the lake.

The Juneberry bushes, sometimes called serviceberries, *Amelanchier alnifolia,* are blooming. The new growth is lightly nibbled by moose. The *Potentilla arguta,* white cinquefoil, are blooming on the marmot's rock, although I haven't seen the marmot this year. He's been reliably at that boulder cluster for years. Wonder what happened to him.

June 23 – We have Barrow's goldeneye with a white crescent. Since I'm new to duck identification and the goldeneyes stay far afield on the opposite side, I've spent a lot of time trying to identify whether this was a common or a Barrow's. But the female tips it off, as she has a fully orange bill while the common female is only tipped with orange. She's with her tiny chicks who are now swimming. Koda and I walked to where I figured her nesting area is. She consistently emerges from that spot with her ducklings when we arrive. Sure enough, she is there with eight ducklings though they are not diving yet. They are really cute, just getting familiar with swimming and staying with mom.

The ring-necked male has a beautiful head and bill. Gleaming black, with a distinctly marked white patch on his side. The female ring-necked ducklings are diving now.

June 29 – We've been arriving very early and hearing sounds like "skew, skew." It was clear these were begging calls from chicks, but the birds must have been hidden in the trees. Chicks that are begging don't abate till they are fed. I recorded the sounds and played them for Dan Hartmann, who is a bird expert and photographer. He said they were most likely great grays. This morning I saw the two chicks, begging incessantly. Fluffy and about 10-12 inches tall. I'll keep my eye out for mom.

July 6 – I arrive early and the lake is perfectly still. From out of a rock comes the bufflehead with tiny ducklings. I haven't seen the male at all. She has a conspicuous white cheek and black head.

After Koda's swim, I visited with the biologists who are collaring grizzlies in the area. They told me the Game and Fish biologists rotate collaring around the Greater Yellowstone, circling back around about every five years. With all the late snows, some of their usual areas have been too difficult to get into. Yet the cliffs above the pond where I spotted grizzly tracks at the end of May are always productive. He said their crew collared a few bears there.

July 10 – 5 p.m. and 78 degrees. Finally feeling like summer has arrived. It's warming up. With the heat, there's another hatch of bugs and they are out in full force. The sedums are blooming. Blue butterflies (possibly blue coppers but my butterfly ID is poor) are out in force. Dragonflies too. Everts thistle or elk thistle, *Cirsium scariosum*, is blooming. You can take a pocket knife, skim off all the thorny leaves and eat the succulent insides. It tastes a bit like celery. The plant is named after Truman Everts. He was a member of the 1870 Washburn-Langford-Doane expedition mapping the area that would later become Yellowstone National Park. Everts wandered off from the expedition, lost his horse with all his supplies, and spent 37 days lost in Yellowstone during the capricious fall season. He attributed his survival to elk thistle, though he weighed only fifty pounds when he was finally found.

Purple small-flowered penstemon is blooming. Sticky geranium with its mass of magenta flowers herald the summer. Masses of small biting flies. No ducks.

July 13 – The biting flies are getting worse. An easterly wind today, which is unusual.

July 23 – I've been arriving very early to avoid the biting flies and mosquitos. Bugs in the evening are unbearable. The black and horse flies are everywhere around the pond. Up until 9 a.m. it's not too bad. Lake still, no breeze. No baby ducks. Ruddy ducks are out there alone. Last week there were no baby ruddy ducklings. No campers since the Nevada couple. A few trucks drive and look and leave. The

Forest Service is beginning to mark the area for winter logging. They will log the south side of the lake where all the blowdowns are. They are targeting the dead and dying Douglas firs on this particular highway for logging since it is a designated scenic highway. The Douglas fir are dying from spruce budworm. Spruce budworm usually doesn't kill trees. The moth lays her eggs on the tree, and when the worms hatch, they mine the tree's new growth. Worms move from bud to bud by a thread of silk webbing, like a spider. If you walk through a heavily infested budworm forest in late spring, you become covered in their webbing. Although we've had a few years of great snow, with intense weeks of cold, that hasn't knocked the budworm back. The firs were already stressed from twenty years of drought and the budworm are sapping the life out of them by eating their developing foliage year after year.

I'm no longer standing at my usual flat rock because the water has risen and is covering it for the first time. The days are very hot. Summers in the mountains are short and buggy.

Usually, Koda emerges with one or two leeches during this time of the year. I've found it's only for a week or two, but this year I haven't seen any. I'm really unclear why leeches have such a short season, and what constitutes the life cycle of a leech. I certainly wouldn't recommend anyone to swim in this lake except a dog.

Driving down the road to the lake is quick and steep. Today a Uinta ground squirrel ran right under my tire before I could stop. Another Uinta is feeding on it already by the time I drive back. They are little cannibals, as my old-timey neighbor likes to tell me.

July 27 – With the moon almost full I decided to go to the lake at night. I park by the highway, and walk down the road. The road is too treacherous to drive at night. With the light of the moon, I see the great gray adult mousing the meadow. She catches a mouse in the field, then her chicks come to investigate. She lets them eat what she's caught. They are observing her actions from a roost in a nearby tree. She's teaching her chicks how to hunt. I sat in the meadow with Koda and watched them for almost a half hour. The curator at the museum told me great grays are very amicable. We didn't seem to spook her at all. What a rare and wonderful sighting.

Aug. 2 – 8:30 a.m. A friend recommended I try putting a life jacket on Koda. He's a good swimmer, but with his impaired breathing and elbow dysplasia, I've sometimes wondered what would happen if he had trouble getting back to shore. I'd have to jump in and save him. The life jacket was a good idea as it keeps him buoyant enough to help his air intake. It's very quiet today with no ducks, but a sudden burst of noise in the nearby woods caught my attention. Two sandhill cranes exploded out of the forest, loudly rattling, then flew directly overhead. Their bugles echoed across the rocky terrain. Yesterday a sandhill was quietly feeding on the ground in the meadow while Koda swam.

Aug. 6 – Barrow's goldeneye with her eight ducklings are swimming and her ducklings are diving now. One grebe and a few unidentified females. The yampah have emerged. The entire meadow is covered in yampah, *Perideridia montana*. Yampah was an important food for Native Americans. In the carrot family, the slender root is small but delicious, a tasty little carrot treat. In all the many years I've come to this pond, I've never seen yampah, but this year the cattle didn't visit the area. Cattle free range and spend a lot of time walking up and down the highway. When they want water, they come into these meadows, trampling the ground and browsing. With a one-year respite, the yampah has returned. I've dug yampah many times and found it very difficult to dig. I usually find it in dry, hard soil or in meadows like this one with the roots entangled amidst the grasses. I've wondered how Native peoples, using only digging sticks, collected yampah. Since it was a major food, and the bulbs are small, they would have to work an entire field. They must have had their sources where the ground was softer, or always worked it after a rain.

Aug. 12 – I was surprised to see a Game and Fish truck when we arrived mid-morning. As Koda's swim was ending, a biologist emerged from the trees where the animal trail to the steep ravine is. He said one of his male grizzlies had already shaken off his GPS collar and he went to retrieve it. Bears like the wide river access and follow it. "That was quick," I thought.

September 23 – Yesterday there was a hunting camp set up with two canvas tents and an electric fence surrounding the campsite.

September 27 – The hunting camp has been here every day, but I still hadn't seen the hunters. I swam Koda for one-half hour, and when we were done, the hunters arrived. They're from Colorado with elk tags. They'd been scouting for several days on the cliffs and the reef above. They told

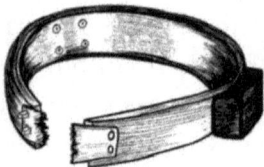

me that in the course of a few days they had two grizzly encounters, or should we say sightings, that were fairly close. Not a surprise as the bears are in hyperphagia, meaning they are hungry, trying to put on winter brown fat for hibernation. The days are getting colder, with occasional snow or rain.

Oct. 1 – Koda didn't make it through October. His throat must have closed up suddenly because he had a difficult time breathing last night. A few days ago, I had a prescient dream. My dream was extremely lucid as if it were real.

I dreamt there is a bear in my bedroom who is hungry. I want to get rid of the bear so I am pushing food down its mouth. After I feed him, the bear is willing to leave. I open the front door to let the bear out, and Koda follows. It's a moonless night, and pitch black outside. As the bear leaves the property, Koda follows him. They walk past the lilacs, down into the pasture, farther and farther. I keep calling "Koda, come," but he doesn't even look back at me. He continues following behind the bear, never glancing back. I awaken and realize it's clear Koda is telling me he is ready to go.

In the morning, Koda is clearly stressed, unable to take a good breath. He rubs against me and I take him outside, hoping he can breathe better. There's been a hoarfrost and the trees are covered in ice. We drive down to the river, a short five minutes away. I walk Koda to the creek where the air is cold with a frost at the water's edge. On any other day, Koda would be in the water. But he is too tired, struggling to catch his breath, and only takes a long look at the place he loves, where he has spent his entire life. The morning is exquisitely beautiful, like an ice palace, with tiny crystals shimmering on the trees. The sky is awakening in vermilion streaks and pale blues. The sudden frost and transformation of the land foretells the change in weather, the passage Koda must now make, and my transition as well. It will be a hard day, but something I know I must do for Koda.

October 6 – I cannot bear to go back to the lake. I take a walk alone after friends leave. Chickadees surrounded me, swarming above my head in the trees. Usually, I see one or two of these friendly little birds, but a swarm is unusual.

October 7 – I head to a wide drainage I've wanted to explore. Koda and I tried to hike this years ago, but there were so many skeleton downed trees left from the 1988 Yellowstone fires that it was too difficult. A snake was laid out in the middle of the road. I stopped and touched it, testing to see if it was dead or just cold. It was warming itself on the road. I gently removed it to the road side. It gave me its strong odor. Snakes symbolically mean change, transition, healing. I thought my encounter was apropos.

I plan to pick up Koda's ashes, then bury them on the hill above my house where he can keep watch and enjoy the view. On my hike, I picked up a deer antler, and gathered white sage for the burial offering. I gave Koda a happy summer of swimming every day, but I think he gave me much more. He gifted me a slowness to observe and appreciate the seasonal changes at the pond, one of his favorite places.

Part II
End of the Wild

WOLVES IN THE CROSSHAIRS

Poaching

Wyoming in October is a weather merry-go-round. Bring several sets of clothing on any given day. A friend who grew up in the 1930s in the valley told me one autumn day he was wrangling horses in the desert, moving them to the mountains. He was wearing short sleeves as the day began, but as he moved the herd up the canyon, he was caught in a freak winter storm, almost dying as the temperatures dropped below zero.

October in my valley is also general deer season. That means any Wyoming resident with a general deer tag from any part of the state can hunt this area. Usually, tags are limited to certain hunt zones, but October in the valley is unique and draws a lot of deer hunters from far and wide. In my area, they are limited to bucks, and since our deer are migratory, arriving from Yellowstone when the snows grow heavy, the bucks are last to arrive, staying high up. But still the hunters come. Early morning before the sun rises, I see their tiny pinpricks light the darkness, circling like flashlights along our dirt road.

I'm leaving in a few days for some out-of-state work. That's why I'm stuffing my daypack for a year-end trek to one of my favorite sites—a Shoshone bighorn sheep trap. Snow flurries and low clouds obscure the horizon, weather that I enjoy, but so do hunters who follow fresh tracks.

The Shoshone sheep trap sits high on a cliff edge with a stunning view of the Absarokas, the mountains that line the eastern margin of Yellowstone Park. The Shoshone in this valley were called Sheep Eaters because of their primary food. They never converted to using horses. Dogs were their preferred companions in this rugged terrain. The dogs could help with the hunt, haul their travois, and be sentinels for enemies. There are still several of these traps concealed in the mountains, posted where large herds of bighorns used to gather. The typical trap is made out of logs shaped in a rectangle, several feet high. A long drive of additional logs, a trap line, fans out from the pen scattered uphill. Along these drive lines, people were stationed, hiding behind trees or boulders, waiting to scare the sheep in the proper direction. Dogs barked and herded the bighorns, while a medicine man assisted with prayers and magic. Sometimes ram horns or skulls are discovered hanging in nearby trees, harnessing extramundane forces and boosting their advantage.

The trap I visit today is rare, and unique, because instead of a log structure, the trap utilizes two immense boulders that form a "V" shape. At the lowest point of the V there is a small opening where a litter of logs, clearly hundreds of years old, are piled to prevent the sheep from escaping. I can walk uphill, and if I am extra observant, the ancient limbs that formed the drive come into view amidst all the ground litter. The logs are out of the ordinary because they clearly line up. Although trees have filled the spaces since the Sheep Eaters used the drive, it doesn't take much to imagine a more open area that pressed the herd into the pen. This particular sheep trap is not just an ingenious use of a natural landform, but it just so happens an animal trail runs right above the trapline. Above are the high meadows the sheep like to use in winter where the wind drifts the snow clear.

For the last two years, the month of October also marked the start of Wyoming's gray wolf hunt. Wyoming wolves were delisted in 2012. The Game and Fish department designated trophy hunt zones bordering the protected lands of Yellowstone and Grand Teton Parks. In their delisting agreement with the federal government throughout the remainder of the state, approximately 85%, wolves were to be labeled as predators. Official "predator status" is simply a modern-day euphemism for "varmint," meaning that animal can be hunted, shot, trapped, or killed anyway you want all year long. That was essentially the status wolves had when they were extirpated from the lower forty-eight in the 1930s. Wyoming pushed hard for varmint status again in the delisting talks with the feds during 2012. They got a major concession, different than any other state with delisted wolves. My hunt zone area borders the eastern boundary of the park where wolves course through year-round from the Lamar Valley, or sometimes from as far away as Idaho. Our packs provide critical genetic infusions for wolves living inside the eastern areas of Yellowstone.

After two years, the wolves secured a stroke of good fortune. Wyoming's wolf hunt was suspended just days before the season was to begin. Environmental groups took Wyoming and the U.S. Fish and Wildlife Service to court and on September 23, a U.S. District Court judge ruled that Wyoming's plan was not sufficient to support a hunt. Wolves went back on the Endangered Species list. Signage was posted, wolf tag dollars refunded, and till further notice wolves could relax. With two years of hunts behind them, the wolves have become very wary of humans, rarely seen, and bolt at even a distant vehicle sound. No hunt means hunters on this October day will not be out looking for a wolf to shoot, and that my dog won't have to wear an orange vest.

Although this bighorn trap is in a remote hidden area, the hike begins at the sole signed trailhead in the valley. It's Saturday and the parking lot is uncharacteristically full. The vehicles belong to deer and elk hunters, yet in years of hiking this trail, I've rarely seen another hiker. On occasion I'll run into a few horsemen, usually in the spring looking for antlers. This is grizzly bear country, and autumn is the time when the bears are hungry, trying to fatten up for hibernation. Hunters draw bears. Only the most experienced, seasoned hunter will venture out on foot up this drainage. The majority of these vehicles are pulling ATV trailers. They intend to drive farther up the road with the hopes of spotting a deer from their vehicle and avoid the struggle of walking. I figure I'll have the trail to myself.

The first mile follows the stream, and then opens to a large confluence where a series of drainages meet in an open meadow. A narrow right-hand gulch is what I want. I move up the dry canyon. To my left, the topography is a gentle slope that divides two valleys. To my right are steep rocky cliffs that house a mesa high above where elk and sheep like to forage in winter. Broken slabs of limestone clutter the hillside. I know the terrain well and begin my climb up the steep hillside near the escarpment edge. Once I get to its flanks, I feel my way like a blind woman along the outcroppings. A narrow gap appears, barely wide enough to slip sideways through. My dog ascends through the crack quickly, but I have to use my hands to pull my weight up beyond a crooked tree that blocks the opening. Loose scree makes the steep terrain difficult to navigate, but it's a short ascent, only thirty feet, and I emerge onto an unexpected narrow shelf. Above the small bench the hill rises steeply, dotted with Douglas firs and pines. An animal trail traffics to a high mesa.

The two house-size boulders sit conspicuously side by side, with a narrow opening between, funneling downhill into the receptacle the Sheep Eaters ingeniously used as a trap. The entire setting encapsulates a strange, numinous beauty, wordlessly expressing the reason why I love this place so much. I've brought a simple offering of some feathers and beads, which I place on the ground, then settle onto the rims to enjoy the view. I'm high above a valley that ascends, then spills into a swath of meadow bordered by forest. I clearly see the ridgeline separating the valley from the one beyond, colored in golds and reds of the turning aspens. I hear no shots, see no hunters, and don't expect to. It's 2:00 in the afternoon. Not the usual time to find game. I'm just luxuriating in the silence and eternal beauty of this mountain vista. I snap a few photos and pull out a snack.

Unexpectedly, two figures appear on the ridgeline. They are dressed in bright orange, and because I am familiar with this area, I know they are coming from what locals dub Dry Lake. I watch them walk slowly, deliberately, over the ridge and down the drainage. I know they cannot see me high on this rib of rock obscured by trees.

I pull out my binoculars to get a closer look as they sit down for a break. Yes, they are definitely hunters because I see their rifles. They rest for about ten minutes, and then continue on their route toward the parking area.

After they leave, I scramble down the terrace and take an alternate route back to my car. When I arrive at the parking lot, the same two hunters are packing up; oddly, they are parked next to my car. It's Wyoming and people are friendly. Outdoorsy folks like to exchange a few stories, at least a few words. But something is off with these two guys. They are unusually quiet. Their eyes deliberately avoid me, and on any other occasion I would have said something first like "see any wildlife?" But they are both absorbed in something, inward, attending to loading the car with a heaviness and a dark mood.

They are a father and son. I rarely see a father hunting with his son. I'm pretty terrible at remembering facial features, but for some reason, maybe just because of their strangeness, I'm drawn to study the two of them. The young man appears to be about thirteen, yet he is tall and gangly for his age. The father is balding, about fiftyish. It's 3 p.m. and they quietly load up their gear, then drive off. It's nice to see a father hunting with his young son, but there is something unsettling about their demeanor. I give it no more thought and in fifteen minutes I'm back at my house, packing for my trip.

By mid-January, I return home to a country blanketed with snow. Coming home from a long trip away, there's always a lot to attend to. I have to turn on the water, check the pipes, warm the cabin up. I notice a business card attached to my front door. It's from the U.S. Fish and Wildlife Senior Special Agent, Office of Law Enforcement.

"Please give me a call—hoping you can help with some information"

I get around to calling Officer Rippeto after a few days, and he informs me of a wolf poaching on the same day I was at the trailhead back in October. He'd been searching for some information since then. He told me the warden rode up on horseback the following morning I was there and found the dead wolf by Dry Lake. He figured he was shot on Saturday.

I asked how he knew I was there that day.

"A Forest Service ranger drove up on Saturday and took down descriptions of all the vehicles parked in the lot. That's routine. The warden recognized your car and told me where you lived. I'd like to come up and take a statement from you."

I told Officer Rippeto that I'd snapped some photos from my view spot. Unfortunately, I didn't take any photos of those hunters. That seemed not only unnecessary and uninteresting, but a bit of an invasion of privacy. Yet I had a time stamp on the pictures, which was moments before they arrived. And, of course, I had a good description of the two fellows.

Several days later, Officer Rippeto came for a visit. He took down my statement. He asked me repeatedly if I remembered their vehicle. What color it was or the general model. I had nothing to say. I showed him my photos and told him my impression of the boy and his father. I didn't hear from him until I called several months later. He told me he was still working on the case but still hadn't found the wolf poachers. I cannot be certain that this father and son were the culprits, but I suspect they were. Rippeto was also suspicious. Their conduct seemed fishy, along with quitting their hunt at an hour when they should be beginning one.

I think about what kind of example that father taught his son. He taught him that poaching was acceptable behavior. And he also gave him the clear message that wolves are not welcome here in Wyoming.

Conservationists lost their fight. After a two-year reprieve, wolves were delisted and hunts began again in the fall of 2017. Wolves learn quickly and after just one season humans returned to their threat list. Yet during those two unhunted years, the valley briefly returned to its baseline, rested in a natural repose of the dance of predator/prey unhindered by man. With the confusion of the court relisting, along with uncertainty as to when a hunt could restart, during those two years when wolves were listed, the U.S. Fish and Wildlife Service wasn't as vigilant as they'd been previously. They collared infrequently in order to cut costs. Collaring involves planes and helicopters with multiple flights and many dead ends. This led to unreliability as to wolf numbers and home ranges. A prominent pack in my area fell off the government's radar. They had no active collars. Occasionally, I'd run into a government official tracking by sight and they'd ask if I'd seen any wolves. Wolf monitoring was reduced to the primitive for two years.

Once the hunts were reinstated, I rarely saw wolves on my hikes. They were no longer curious about humans. One day in late spring, when the light is low and dusk lingers for hours, I headed out after dinner for a short hike in a series of craggy volcanic contours of hills and narrow arroyos. Some of these gullies hold snow melt runoff for weeks, attracting bears and cougars. I thought I'd place a trail camera along one. Following a narrow animal trail over slippery scree slopes, I settled on a tight channel with a trickle of water running through it. The approaching slopes were steep. I set up the camera in the gully, and as I headed back up the slope to the makeshift trail, a wolf came trotting down. We saw each other simultaneously, less than ten feet apart. I relished the moment, but she didn't. Startled, she jolted, eyed me for less than a moment, then darted off. It was the last time I encountered a wolf so close after the hunts began.

Harassment

With Tom bailing due to work, my Wind River Mountains backpacking trip was going to be solo. I've done plenty of solo backpacks, and after twenty years of exploring the Winds, I feel pretty comfortable on my own. I've gotten soft when it comes to mosquitos, and the Wind Rivers are known for their abundance. In fact, they are an integral part of the summer landscape. By planning my Wind River trips in September, I avoid the bugs, but that also enables me to explore marshy areas. Labor Day weekend might bring an early snow that pushes the visitors out as well, leaving the backcountry pristine.

This September was unique. Fires were raging throughout Montana all summer. Wyoming had been spared, but the smoke was blowing south, covering the mountain ranges for over a month. Driving en route through Jackson, the Tetons were absent on the horizon. I thought the Winds might escape the smoke being farther southeast, but I was mistaken. The craggy flanks of the Continental Divide, the Winds' claim to fame, were barely visible.

This year I picked out a small area I'd never been to. Although it's close to popular Titcomb Basin, Chain Lakes is mainly used as a pass-through to the middle Winds. Chain Lakes is comprised of a series of two large oblong lakes separated by a narrow outlet that is rock hoppable. The lakes lie in an enormous rocky basin at lower elevation than the high divide that is the popular destination for hikers. Since the lakes are a two-day destination hike, I assumed I'd see few visitors. From there I could day hike up to a cirque of lakes below Mt. Baldy.

Elkhart Park trailhead is a short, mostly paved road from Pinedale. Entrances to trailheads in the Winds are generally long and rough over washboard dirt roads. Because of the easy access to Elkhart Park, the trailhead draws a flood of day hikers and backpackers. I was lucky. The lot wasn't full when I arrived at 3 p.m. I decided to hike the five miles to Sweeny Lake, hoping to arrive before dark. People were pouring out, presumably from the popular Titcomb Basin after the Labor Day weekend.

The Elkhart trail follows a wooded ridge for five miles before it splits to either Titcomb Basin or Pole Creek, an otherwise nondescript trek except for the evidence of beetle-kill. I hiked this trail eight years ago up to Lester Pass. The whitebark pines were healthy then. Now they are a sad scene, the Winds being one of the last strongholds for these trees in the Greater Yellowstone. Most are dead or dying.

Sweeny and Miller lakes lie in an open bowl below the ridgeline and add only an extra half mile, well worth it since there's no water until Elklund lake—a popular campsite destination that might be overcrowded. With the shorter days and the light closing in, I make the decision to head downhill toward the two lakes. Upper Sweeny is an isolated gem set within rocky knobs with good camping spots. An orange full moon rises, with the high peaks obscured from the fires raging across the West. A bugling elk breaks my early morning silence.

Chain Lakes, my base camp destination, is another seven miles. The trail traverses a rocky glaciated landscape, passing through granite knolls till it reaches the crossing at Pole Creek. At the crossing I pause for a snack on a rock hidden in the willows off trail. A deer bursts from the woods, down the trail, pauses at the creek till it spies me, then barrels through the wide creek crossing. Moments later, an outfitter appears with two mules who had obviously spooked the deer. We chat for a few moments. He's headed for his wall tent camp to pick up supplies. It's not hunting season yet. He's packing supplies for hikers that don't want to carry their own loads. He'll pack in food, but also chairs and other amenities, possibly gear for those climbing Gannett Peak via Titcomb.

This man would be the last person I'd see for days. Hikers prefer to use the higher elevation Fremont Trail that hugs the granite peaks. I take off my boots, ford the wide stream, and ascend a faulted narrow valley teeming with willows and a wet tread. I reach a low rise, and the viewscape opens south into the impressive broad basin of Chain Lakes. Marshy ground choked with willows feeds like amorphous fingers outward from the lakes. The trail skirts the bogs following the northeast shore on higher dry ground by the forest's edge. I keep my eye out for used fire rings and an open campsite area with good water, but it appears no one uses this as a stop-over. The broad vista down the wide basin allows me to see someone camped or traveling over a mile away, but I see no one. A lonely, ignored place. I leave the hillside, walk through the wet stunted willows over to a small rise that looks like a potential site. The rise has wind protection with conifers and is conveniently located directly above the upper lake's outlet. I camp on the lee side, but I can easily walk around the slope to the narrow rocky outlet for water. A forested hill on the opposite side can provide firewood. Dusk is settling in. The smoke from the Montana fires paints a white glow around the spires of the surrounding peaks. I fill my water bottle at the muddy outlet between the two large lakes and notice elk, wolf, and moose tracks.

The following morning the air feels cool and crisp with perfect fall weather. My plan is to make a quick breakfast then day hike to Mt. Baldy lakes. I prepare my oatmeal, then walk to the top of the rise to eat with a view. I've spent many days and nights in the Wind Rivers, usually above 10,000 feet in the granite terrain of stunted trees and glacial lakes. Few animals live here. So when my morning breakfast was interrupted by the howl of wolves, I was elated. The chorus begins across from my campsite, centered in the wooded hillside. I circle the small rise and find an optimal rock from which to view the woods and listen. I don't see any wolves as they are hidden in the trees. Their song carries like an echo through the valley. I can hear several wolves in the trees signaling to a responsive call farther down the southern Chain Lake. Although the Winds are not known to have many wolves, they are slowly making their way in. The problem is that much of the western front, areas where deer and elk overwinter, is in the predator zone where wolves are not protected. I've heard wolves singing twice before in the Wind River Mountains. Once on the Reservation side, and much farther south near Washakie Park. But this was the closest I'd heard them in the Winds, just a few hundred yards away. Their night hunt was ending and they were gathering back together.

As I munched on my oatmeal, listening to wolves, another sound pierced the air. I recognize it from all the collaring carried out in my valley in January. A fixed-wing spotter plane emerges into view, heading directly for the wolves' knoll. As the plane descends, I become more confused. I know I'm in a wilderness area. Why is there a plane at less than 500 feet here? Is this a private plane, a wealthy person sightseeing? I've never been disturbed by low-flying planes in wilderness areas except if they are on a search and rescue mission. What are the rules for planes in wilderness?

The plane is closing in till it's barely above the treetops. Then it begins circling above the trees, clearly trying to flush the wolves. Game and Fish, while flying for wildlife spotting and collaring in my area, use yellow planes. Collaring wolves occurs in winter, when wolves are packed up and snow makes them easy to spot. Clearly this pilot is not collaring, but he's picked up the GPS signal from a collared wolf in the pack. Hacking coordinates off a collar is not that difficult for someone in the know. Now I'm confused—am I in the predator or the trophy zone? Hunts in the trophy zone don't start until October. And using a plane to spot wildlife after July 31 is illegal, including wolves in the predator zone.

The fine print of all these questions is not foremost in my mind. Right now, this guy is disturbing my peace, along with harassing these wolves. I've just hiked fifteen miles into wilderness to enjoy a quiet breakfast and some howls, and he's violating my tranquility and calm. By now I'm standing, yelling, jumping up and down to catch his attention and giving him the middle finger. I know he cannot hear me, but he certainly can see my furious gestures. After six tight passes skimming the treetops, the plane departs, heading south along lower Chain Lake. The animals never flushed but they certainly silenced. I'm mad, perplexed, and confused by all I just witnessed. I pack up for my day hike and head for Baldy Lakes.

The trail to Baldy Lakes rings Mt. Baldy, gaining 500 feet in a mile and a half. It's a fine trail, although muddy in spots. Black bear, deer, moose, elk, and wolf prints are abundant. The route climbs steeply through dense forest then spills into boggy meadows with an abundance of water from the high lakes. Baldy Lakes are a series of small alpine lakes leading to a waterfall. A feeder trail merges with the Fremont Trail.

From the lakes I decide to cross-country back to my campsite, making a loop that crisscrosses the opposite side of Mt. Baldy. I follow the ridgelines and open areas where I encounter the outfitter's tent camp about halfway below. He's not there, and an electric fence line encircles the canvas tent. I locate his horse trail for easy passage and follow it for a while. The horse trail leads back to the western bench toward Pole Creek, so I need to zig-zag south to my campsite.

The following morning, the wolves are back, this time without the spotter plane. I enjoy their serenade undisturbed. After they disperse, I'm still pondering what was that plane all about, what was its purpose here? If I hadn't been there, would they have poached those wolves? Looking for clues, I decide to explore the hillside where the wolves gathered. Possibly I'd discover why this was their rendezvous site. I cross the creek and head up the slope. The forest floor is easy to walk through. An old growth forest open underneath. The hillside is not too steep with plenty of stock evidence. Using an animal trail, I run into something completely unexpected—a mule carcass about two or three weeks old. Bones are scattered, indicating canines have been eating their fill. It's picked clean but not yet leathery. That must be why the wolves were still visiting this site, using it as their morning rendezvous.

Seeing the carcass, my mind is now racing. The only livestock grazing here are outfitters passing the night. All the grazing allotments along the west front of the Winds are long retired. The last allotment to be retired was a few years ago—a sheep allotment in the southern Winds. Paranoia starts to set in, and now I'm forming a variety of stories in my mind. Did the outfitter who ran the tent camp shoot an old mule here? That's a real possibility. Old horses and mules that can't make it back are shot in the backcountry. Or did he do it just to lure the wolves, and then to shoot them? Wolves are such a focus of enmity in Wyoming I would not put it past an outfitter that makes his living bringing clients in for the fall elk hunt. To him, these wolves are competition. If I am in the predator zone, he'd be in his legal right to bait and shoot, but not from a plane. Or was this plane intending to poach wolves, an outfitter or someone else with illegal access to the coordinates?

I have too many questions, and I've created a tangled sinister story to fill in the blanks. I spend a few more days exploring the beautiful basin, my evenings and mornings punctuated by howls, then head out to camp at Eklund Lake, which in retrospect I do not recommend. My plan is to leave Eklund before daybreak and catch the sunrise from Photographer's Point. I arrive at the Point a half hour before sunrise. The mountains are still shrouded in smoke like a Chinese ink drawing. The air is perfectly still. The moon lies low in the heavens as a cerulean sky reveals the rising sun. There is no wind, yet I hear the wind. It is coming from below in the canyon. A deep roar, like a howling gale, barrels down the Fremont Creek drainage from the Divide's numerous lakes and alpine peaks. Time flows in glacial epochs as rivers roar beneath me. The Wind Rivers. After twenty years of hiking here and pondering that beautiful poetic name, I now understood its origin. The rivers roar like the wind. Maybe it is the allure of this sound that continually draws me back year after year to this place I love so deeply. The wolves are back; the mountains are singing their windy songs. Things are right again.

After my confusing experience with wolves, a plane, and the carcass, I head to Jackson for a visit to the Wyoming Game and Fish office. As I suspected, Chain Lakes sits barely within the trophy zone. Although a recommendation, not a rule, the Aeronautics Information Manual (AIM) says: "pilots are requested to maintain a minimum altitude of 2,000' above the surface of the following: *National Parks, Monuments, Seashores, Lakeshores, Recreation Areas and Scenic Riverways administered by the National Park Service, National Wildlife Refuges, Big Game Refuges, Game Ranges and*

Wildlife Ranges administered by the U.S. Fish and Wildlife Service, and Wilderness and Primitive areas administered by the U.S. Forest Service."

I run into WGF biologist Dan Thompson who tells me he'll check on the situation and get back to me. A few weeks later I receive an email from Game and Fish informing me the pilot was *"locating wolves to demonstrate recovery."* That sounded too officious so I contact Ken Mills, the wolf biologist at the Pinedale office. Ken tells me the plane I saw was contracted out of Dubois to search for grizzly bears. The pilot picked up the signal from the wolves and decided to check that out as well. That calmed all my muddle of thoughts about poaching. But the question still remained. While all this was legal, should we consider it ethical, or even necessary? Clearly this was harassment of these wolves, even though they were not collaring, which is also not permitted in wilderness. Whether in wilderness or not, pushing wildlife with mechanical devices stresses them. When wildlife agencies conduct collaring efforts, the loss of a few animals is expected. Running wildlife, especially in warm weather, can easily lead to exhaustion.

All this begs the question: what exactly is wilderness for? First and foremost, wilderness areas were created to protect wildlife, especially while breeding and using preferred habitat. If keeping a flight distance at 2,000 feet is a request, and not a Federal Aviation Regulations rule, then what prevents poachers and random tourist flights into wilderness? Of course, another obvious reason for wilderness protections is the human one: peace and quiet to enjoy the natural beauty and sounds of nature.

In the early days of radio collaring and tracking, no one knew it would eventually be used to monitor for predator control. It's disingenuous to say these wolves were being monitored to demonstrate recovery, when in reality they are tracked to set hunt quotas. Even though Game and Fish can legally fly into any area for wildlife monitoring (they are not allowed to set down a helicopter in wilderness), does that mean they should? We could have monitoring going on all year long deep in wilderness areas with low-flying drones or planes.

Technological wildlife monitoring is now at disturbing levels. We track and follow wildlife to such a degree that our definition of wildlife management has crossed over to *wildlife husbandry*. The fear that poachers or hunters could hack GPS coordinates is real, confirmed to me by a Forest Service biologist. Trail cameras, aircraft, illegal grabs of GPS coordinates, over-snow vehicles, powerful long-range rifles and scopes—wildlife using only their senses don't have a chance. We need to ask our agencies, and ourselves, where does all this monitoring begin and end?

GRIZZLIES IN A WINDOWLESS ROOM

"**H**is cowboy boots are probably still sitting there."

Kirk was relating the story of J.K. Rollinson, the first Forest Service ranger in the valley where I live. Rollinson helped build a government cabin in the Beartooth Mountains in 1908. My new friend Kirk, a slight man in his mid-80s yet still in excellent shape, had guided me the week before to another historic Beartooth site—a crumbling stockade from the 1860s hidden within a copse of spruce. Kirk grew up in the Big Horn basin where he worked in an array of outdoor jobs throughout his life, including with the Forest Service. The cabin, he said, if it's still there, was at Sparhawk Lake.

I knew the Beartooth Range pretty well, but hadn't heard of Sparhawk. Kirk said the lake was named after Ranger Frank Sparhawk. Sparhawk, along with Rollinson, used the cabin as a summer refuge while overseeing livestock operations in this high alpine environment. The small cabin saved the rangers a ten-mile rugged horseback trip from the Crandall Ranger Station. I was curious if any remnants were left. Poring over a map, I found the tarn not far from Sawtooth Lake, a large body of water wrapped at the base of a mountain bearing the same name. A rough dirt road off the main highway leads to Sawtooth's lakefront. The road is in good shape for the first mile and a half, then turns into a rocky, rutted mess. I pulled off where the road loses its shape and walked the final two and a half miles to the lake.

Spruce and whitebark pine forest, interspersed with verdant meadows of high alpine wildflowers, make this scenic dirt access road a popular weekend ride for off-roaders. The course is along a ridgeline overlooking a U-shaped wetland of marsh and lakes. The adjacent eastern ridgeline, visible at times from the Sawtooth road, is also a popular route. Called the Morrison Jeep Road, it's a historic trail used as a connector route from the 10,000-foot Beartooth Plateau down to the desert mouth of the Clark's Fork Canyon. The local ATV club was anxious for a loop trail joining Sawtooth Lake with the Jeep trail. To accomplish that, the Forest Service would have to build a new road into and through the marsh up to the opposite ridgeline. That was another reason I wanted to walk this road: I had to see what kind of habitat damage that would create.

A few hundred yards before the final approach to Sawtooth Lake, I encountered a parked Toyota 4-Runner with Montana plates. That last stretch is too rough and eroded for even the toughest vehicle. I also heard gunshots. It was early September, not yet hunting season, but these fellows were using trees for target practice on the far side of the lake. I couldn't see them, but sure could hear their antics. No one else was around, and thankfully the route to Sparhawk was in the opposite direction.

I found the remains of Sparhawk's cabin—a small jewel hidden within dense tree cover—by the side of the lake, along with a Forest Service plaque commemorating his service. Only the log outline of a tiny cabin, but no cowboy boots, remained. I ate lunch, then returned the route I came. Walking the road back up the steep hill, I found the 4-Runner still parked on the small knoll. From this point, the road opens into a meadow edged with dense tree cover on its far side. Breaking the forest's silence, a deep sonorous barking suddenly roared through the trees. I stopped and listened. The mysterious low-pitched "honk" came again, then again. I looked across the meadow just in time to see a large grizzly bear running through the woods, followed by a tiny cub. The barking continued and another cub ran to catch up with her bear mother. These little cubs, born last winter, referred to as cubs of the year or COY for short, were incredibly cute.

All this ruckus was far enough away, with me downwind, that I wasn't afraid. Mom was headed for the lake at a quick clip. The barking continued, like an old man with a wheezy cough and a megaphone, and after a few minutes, a third cub appeared.

Mesmerized by this scene, I momentarily forgot about the men still down by the lake who were probably fishing by now. Instead, I reflected on the increasing use by grizzlies of this alpine area. The Beartooths are good habitat with intact whitebark pines—now a rarity in the rest of the ecosystem due to widespread beetle kill. Females who eat whitebark pine nuts are known to have larger litters. Here was a successful grizzly mother utilizing these resources.

When the bears were out of sight, I remembered the men. No chance for me to let them know those bears were on their way toward them. The quartet of bears would be at lakeside before I could even turn around. I hoped the men would not run into them, or at the very least keep their cool. I assumed they had bear spray. Most people around here know to carry it while in the backcountry. And then I had one horrible thought. These men had guns, and possibly were a bit trigger-itchy for opening season. I hoped the worst didn't happen.

As I hiked the road back to my car, I had a lot on my mind. This was not my first grizzly sighting of the summer in the Beartooth Mountains, but my third. More grizzlies were moving into these high mountains. Just a few weeks ago I ran into a different mother with a cub while backpacking. Earlier in the summer, my dog Koda spooked a young bear napping behind a large boulder. But unlike those other encounters, Sawtooth Lake is a high human-use area. And now the ATVers were pressuring the Forest Service for an additional loop through the swamp below. That would inevitably bring more traffic, more picnickers, more trash. Studies have shown that grizzlies are disturbed by roads and vehicular traffic. Not only was I worried about the disturbance to the bears in their newly occupied summer range, but the Beartooth Range is summer habitat for elk and wolves as well. Easier access means more people deeper into the backcountry, and more disturbance to wildlife.

Later that same week, I was on a group hike accompanied by Shoshone Forest Service bear biologist Andy Pils. I told him about my bear encounter at Sawtooth and he had new information for me.

"Just as that mother grizzly arrived by the lakeshore, the Montana fellows were walking around the lake to pick up the road to their car. When they saw the sow—although they reported seeing only two cubs—they completely freaked out, dropped their packs along with their fishing tackle and rods, and ran back to their car. Worse, they threw down a cooler full of food. Then high-tailed it back to their home in Billings."

Once back in the city, Pils told me, the men mulled over their encounter and all the junk they'd left at the lakeshore. Instead of thinking about the food reward they'd left those bears, "these guys thought that people finding their stuff strewn around might believe the bear ate them, so they called the Forest Service to report they were still alive and told me what happened."

When Pils learned they'd left their cooler there, he told them that was a huge mistake. Those young cubs got a major food reward. That would be something they'd never forget. An association with people and food had been instilled in those COY.

It was apparent the Montana fellows had little preparation for recreating in grizzly habitat. They defended their decision to drop the cooler ("But it was a thousand-pound grizzly!") and asked Pils if he could retrieve their stuff for them. ("We broke an axle getting out of there.")

Of course, grizzlies in the Yellowstone ecosystem do not get up to a thousand pounds. More likely, this mother bear was about three hundred pounds. Pils also told me these guys had no bear spray. It took Pils two trips to clean things up. The bears had demolished the cooler, eaten all the food, and thrown the trash all around, but the fishing tackle and backpacks were intact.

The incident at Sawtooth Lake painted a picture of the many obstacles grizzlies, and other wildlife, face in the Greater Yellowstone area—the influx of tourists and new locals who are unfamiliar with proper protocol in bear country, plus the pressures from interest groups for new access roads that encroach upon wildlife and bring more people deeper into pristine areas.

The following spring, I attended a U.S. Fish and Wildlife Service (USFWS) meeting in Cody. This is a formal meeting to discuss whether the Service should delist the grizzly bear after over forty years of protections on the Endangered Species list. A woman greets me at the meeting room entrance and asks if I want to speak. I sign up and find a seat. The meeting begins and in short order the roll call of public commentators commences. An older man walks to the podium, gives his name to the secretary, and has two minutes to speak his peace. He lives outside of town in an unincorporated area at the mouth of the Clark's Fork Canyon, a sagebrush rocky terrain where the locals used to have an open dump.

"My wife is afraid to take a walk down the road," he begins. "We have too many bears coming in. It's time to delist and have a hunt." What he doesn't report is that locals are still dumping their animal carcasses behind a knoll I stumbled upon last year.

Another older man takes his turn at the microphone. "I'm afraid to go horseback riding in the forest." The element of fear colors the rationale on whether to delist or not. It's not clear if people are seeing more grizzlies because there really are more, or if bears are descending farther off the mountains seeking new food sources, having lost whitebark pine nuts as their fall larder.

It's my turn to speak. I state that I live in a drop-off place for problem bears. My valley has one of the highest

concentrations of grizzlies in the Greater Yellowstone—
"every drainage is occupied, but with a bit of effort, we can
co-exist," I say. "Grizzlies are minders-of-their-own-busi-
ness." I am speaking for the bear, but mostly for my own
peace of mind. I know the Service is driven not just by
science, but by political pressures. That tenuous line of recovery is in the eye of the beholder.

The Interagency Grizzly Bear Study Team says the bear
is "recovered" and therefore we must delist. But what is
their yardstick? With the bears occupying less than 2% of
their historic habitat, humans are essentially saying enough
is enough. We will only tolerate seven hundred bears and
they must stay confined to this tiny "island" that we circum-
scribed and call the Demographic Monitoring Area.

The bears don't care about any of this. It's human business.
If I were to ask a bear, they'd probably tell me they've already
greatly accommodated us humans. There are no bear representatives at this meeting. The biologists are not advocating
for the bears. Their job is to count numbers, then present those
statistics. The audience seems divided between those who
fear a bear is lurking around every tree, and those who love
to admire bears from cars. It is the rare individual who deeply
knows and understands grizzly bear consciousness, and those
bear whisperers, if they even exist, are not here. Meanwhile,
I cannot help but reflect on the incongruity that grizzlies are
busy living their lives—minding their own business—while
we sit in a windowless room deciding their fate.

In the end, the USF&W pushed ahead and delisted the
bear, adding grizzlies to the list of trophy hunted predators,
along with wolves, black bears, and mountain lions.

Before the USFWS delisted the grizzly in the Greater Yellowstone Region, Wyoming Game and Fish was having their own meetings, supposedly gauging public opinion. During these meetings, the subject of hunting was off-limits. The meetings were staged as if Wyoming Game and Fish hadn't yet made any decisions about a hunt, as if they might be considering the delisted bear like bald eagles—no longer an Endangered Species but not a hunted animal. Everyone knew this was pure optics.

During our local meeting, I was camping in Utah, but fortunately I was able to race back to attend the last scheduled public meeting, which took place in Jackson. While waiting for the meeting to begin, I stood outside the meeting room chatting with a Game and Fish employee. We were interrupted by a large, older man, who swaggered over wearing a black cowboy hat. Accompanying him were several younger fellows, also wearing black cowboy hats. This man exchanged a few words, then went into the hall. The "black hats" all sat together in the front of the hall. During the comment period, the senior black hat made it known he was hostile to bears and his ranching livelihood depended upon their delisting and a hunt.

May rolled around for the final Game and Fish Commission meeting, which would determine whether the delisted bears would be hunted. Representatives from all the major conservation groups, along with a few members of the public who were against a grizzly hunt, showed up at the Holiday Inn in Lander to advocate for, at a minimum, a five-year moratorium on a grizzly hunt. I considered wearing my black cowboy hat, but the black hats didn't show. They already knew the outcome.

The Game and Fish department was proposing killing up to twenty-two bears with a sixty-day season. It's impossible to tell a female from a male bear, unless you see cubs. So the proposal said if one female was killed within the DMA, the area where bears are counted toward the population, the hunt would be shut down. I knew the Wyoming Commissioners would sanction the hunt. Wyoming Game and Fish is driven by a hunting mentality, and the opportunity to hunt grizzly bears after a forty-year hiatus was in their crosshairs for years. Once approved, the fee was $15 to be entered into a lottery. If your name was selected, then it was $600 for in-state, $6,000 for an out-of-state tag. Out of the blue, a campaign was initiated called "Shoot 'em with a Camera," as opposed to a gun. The campaign started a fund to help anyone with the money who might draw a tag, and pretty soon hundreds of people were paying the $15 lottery fee who had no intention of killing a bear. Since the Game and Fish rules mandated only ten hunters could be in the DMA zone at a time with a ten-day limit, anyone that succeeded in getting a tag and not killing a bear only needed to hike around during those ten days. Out of over seven thousand applicants, two conservation advocates won a tag. Ironically, one of those coveted tags went to Tom Mangelson, wildlife photographer and well-known grizzly bear advocate, who had spoken against the hunt at the recent Commissioner's meeting. Hunters cried foul, but under state rules, if you pay for a tag, you are legal. One's intentions to kill or not makes no difference. Besides, not every hunt is successful. Since few people would draw tags, and there was a short season, the idea of Shoot 'Em with a Camera was to limit the number of bears killed, running the clock out.

The tribes too had geared up for this day. Over a hundred tribal groups and nations signed the Piikani Grizzly Treaty condemning hunting an animal they considered sacred and demanding continued federal protections of the bear. Their request was ignored by the USFWS. The tribes sued the Service, as did conservation groups. Just days before the hunt was to begin, U.S. District Judge Dana Christensen restored ESA protections, saying the USFWS couldn't "balkanize" bear populations in different regions, delisting each one in turn. That was September 2018. In May 2020, the USFWS and Wyoming lost their appeal, with the bears still protected as of this writing.

When Senator Daines from Montana asked Rep. Deb Haaland during her committee confirmation hearing for Secretary of the Interior Department why she co-sponsored legislation to "keep the grizzly bear on the Endangered Species List forever," he mischaracterized the bill. The bill Haaland co-sponsored with Rep. Raúl Grijalva was the Tribal Heritage and Grizzly Bear Protection Act. That bill would have protected grizzlies from hunting (except in certain cases of conflict and tribal religious ceremonies), even when they were delisted, decoupling the two. It also reiterated the request to relocate grizzlies to suitable habitat within historic ranges on tribal lands.

The sound argument against delisting is several-fold: grizzlies in the Greater Yellowstone need connection with the bears in the Northern Rockies to maintain genetic diversity; bears need connectivity to find viable food sources as their principal foods are compromised in the Yellowstone area; and climate change is the great unknown when it comes to food and habitat. Additionally, the USFWS still hasn't fulfilled their stated goals when the bear was put on the ESA, which was to have five viable bear populations in the Northern Rockies.

Bears will move to find other bears and new food sources over time. With around 1,800 grizzlies in the Northern Rockies, all this could be accomplished without ESA protections now, but *only* if delisting is *permanently* decoupled from hunting. Grizzlies need to be protected in perpetuity. That would take a Congressional Act.

We have lost our stories about the Great Bear. Grizzlies deserve more than people sitting inside windowless rooms debating whether a hunt should begin again. Our only modern stories of bears revolve around our fears. People for thousands of years sat around campfires and told tales and myths about bears. Bears eat similar foods as humans, are highly intelligent, have an aura of power and presence, and in their hibernation, they represent the mystery of death and rebirth. To our ancestors, bears were numinous and mysterious beings. We need new stories, not just the stories of how to use bear spray or electric fencing. With new stories, we can form an alliance that ensures the bear's survival, as well as fosters their expansion.

During the COVID summer of 2020, a friend and I walked the potholed road to Sawtooth Lake. Before the road turned too nasty, campers and travel trailers filled every flat space, even beyond the legal limit. When we arrived at the lake, there were a few tent campers and fishermen. With the influx of more and more people, grizzlies will have less space and there will be more opportunities for human conflicts.

The Greater Yellowstone along with the Northern Rockies is a special place. I confess that when I leave and visit other beautiful landscapes in the West—and there are many—the land harbors a loneliness without grizzly bears or wolves. It's a tangible and felt absence, a hole in the natural fabric that once weaved all of nature's parts together. It is imperative to preserve this vulnerable landscape along the Northern Rockies spine. For those who want to recreate here, for those who want to escape urban life and move here, the cautious advice isn't to carry bear spray. The cautious advice is that we must endeavor to preserve habitat and tolerance for the last of our grizzlies.

Coyote: The Fall Guy

March 2019

few weeks ago, our Wyoming Game and Fish (WGF) local ungulate biologist held a public meeting to discuss the startling decline in our mule deer numbers. We've had several hard winters in a row, the worst being 2016-2017, with a winter snowpack that locals hadn't seen in over forty years. That winter was so tough on our mule deer that when spring emerged, the number of dead deer across the landscape was staggering. I personally witnessed this. I saw deer that clearly just lay down and died—under trees, in wooded slot canyons, along wildlife trails. There were dead deer no predators had ever touched, with only their eyes pecked out. On spring hikes exploring gullies and draws, there was a dead deer every quarter mile. Some of these deer were scavenged, but the sheer volume of carcasses was beyond what even scavengers could quickly clean up. I photographed bears fresh from their winter dens so fat they looked like they were going into hibernation, rather than emerging from it. It was clear to anyone who lived here that three years of intense winters had taken an enormous toll on our deer population.

This winter 2018-2019, our snowpack has been light, but February was intensely cold. Few daytime temperatures cracked zero. The extreme weather was especially hard on fawns trying to make it through their first winter. The word from WGF is that our herd objective or carrying capacity, an estimate of the population the land and vegetation can tolerate, is four thousand to six thousand. But their estimate is the herd has been reduced to 2,900. Nearby, another hunt area's target objective of 9,600-14,400 has a herd estimated at 6,900. And, according to Game and Fish, the decline began even two years before the winter of 2016-2017.

I was curious as to what actions the agency would take. I knew they wouldn't sit back and do nothing. The night the meeting was scheduled I was snowed in. So the next morning I called Game and Fish biologist Tony Mong. Mong came to Cody from Dixon where he had on-the-ground experience working with the Wyoming Migration Initiative, a statewide project that was tracking elk, deer, and pronghorn migrations.

Starting in 2016, WGF began collaring deer in our mountain valley to track their movement. What they found amazed everyone.

I'd noticed for years that in the spring deer steadily gathered into increasingly larger groups. Then, one day like clockwork, they'd all disappear. I assumed they headed for the bowl of mountains that surrounded the valley, yet except for the few resident deer that stayed in the nearby woods, I never encountered deer on summer hikes. I wasn't the only one who was perplexed. Through the collaring project, researchers were astonished to learn of this herd's long migration, along with several other herds along the eastern front of Yellowstone. One collared deer was tracked as far away as Hayden Valley, a journey over fifty airline miles traversing rugged terrain. Deer follow the green-up, then remain in the high country until the fall snows force them down. In September, the does and fawns begin to reappear. The bucks follow a bit later. This herd undertakes one of the longest deer migrations in Wyoming.

Mong acknowledged the hard winters were a major factor in the decline. He also told me that these two herds have never been robust. The collaring revealed why—their long migrations. That alone takes its toll. I asked Mong if there had been a study on the low doe-to-fawn ratio to determine all factors. "Not yet."

The week following my conversation with Mong, I noticed snowmobile tracks behind a locked Forest Service gate just off the main highway. This dirt road is closed to all vehicle traffic in winter. Prime elk winter habitat on a high plateau at the road's end is the reason. There is one small inholding within the alpine meadows; otherwise, the entire area is National Forest. Someone either had a key with permissions, or they'd cut the lock and were trespassing.

I decided to follow the tracks on foot. The expansive meadows several miles up were once part of a homestead and this was the wagon route. Now it's just a steep, pot-holed, unmaintained four-wheel drive. In winter the snow can be deep. With snowshoes it took me over an hour to reach the plateau. Once there, the expanse is vast, rimmed with views of the surrounding peaks. This is high country where the winds sweep the snow clean, meadows that bull elk prize in winter months. Since it was early April, male bears could also be emerging. I did see a set of iced-over grizzly tracks on the way up.

I was still following the snowmobile tracks. They were leading to the inholding at the far end of the meadow. I wondered who those tracks belonged to. The cabin's owner would have no reason to come up during winter. She ran cattle in the summer, using the cabin infrequently. The cabin was part of the original homestead and quite rustic—not a place to stay in a lonesome valley in winter. Something else was happening here.

The next week, my friend Don arrived at my house for a visit. He'd been searching for antlers, sometimes called shed or horn hunting. He likes to spend his days hiking, and picking up antlers can be good money. The antler business has taken off since they started using them for dog chews and in Chinese quack medicine cures. Some of his favorite haunts were the forested hillsides that encircled the high meadows. He'd just returned from walking up the same road where the snowmobiles had been. Don told me he saw piles of meat on the private inholding, that he'd run into the fellows driving the snowmobiles who said they were working for Wildlife Services. Wildlife Services is a completely misnamed government agency that uses various methods to kill wildlife, particularly in the service of ranchers, farmers, and hunters. The snowmobiles were hauling drums of meat, used as bait for coyotes.

Now I was really concerned. I'd seen Wildlife Services flying in the desert looking for coyotes. I'd even known a man who briefly worked for Wildlife Services. He disgusted me when he boasted of killing over 400 raccoons one summer, "varmints" that were eating farmers' corn fields. But we don't have problems with coyotes in the mountains. Cattle are hauled in for summer grazing, then hauled out by truck in the fall. Wildlife Services doesn't have any jurisdiction over grizzly bears, which do kill cattle occasionally. And although Wildlife Services will kill wolves, it is highly regulated, requiring Game and Fish sign-off with a carcass inspection. They do not pre-treat an area for wolves, even in Wyoming's wolf predator zone.

I called Mong once again and asked what was going on. Coyotes, being listed as predators in Wyoming, are not under the purview of Game and Fish. Whatever was being done here, he said, was independent and under the jurisdiction of Wildlife Services. Mong said Wyoming Game and Fish would normally only sanction controls where deer birth their fawns. It's the newborns who are the most vulnerable to predation of any kind, not just coyotes. But in this case, these deer are fawning during their migration, either in the park or in wilderness, places where Wildlife Services cannot do controls. Their best shot, he said, was to pre-treat by killing coyotes in my valley, even though these coyotes wouldn't be the same coyotes who would be the fawn killers.

None of this made any sense, at least scientific sense. But I assumed it was all a PR stunt, something the agency could tell sportsmen who were upset about the low deer numbers. If they called a public meeting to announce low mule deer numbers in specific hunt areas, it took no great leap of intellect to know that meant a reduced mule deer quota next fall for hunters. Hunters are quick to blame predators. Predators are nature's competition for hunters. The agency could say, "We're on it. Coyotes are being hunted down."

I decided to dig deeper. I wanted to speak with the Wildlife Services supervisor for my district. Quickly I discovered there was no listing for the local office. Finding a government agency should be easy, considering we support it with our tax dollars. I got the address from a friend in the Forest Service. I drove there but only found an abandoned office with no signage. There was a listed number for the central office in Casper. They gave me a local number, which I called. Unexpectedly, a man named Mike answered and said he'd meet me in ten minutes at a different address. That address was a storage facility. Clearly, this government agency was quite clandestine, keeping as low a profile as possible. I waited at the curb until I saw a man drive up and walk inside an unmarked door.

Mike was a friendly, personable fellow. Short, fit, he was talkative and open. His so-called office was a tiny room, disheveled, indicating he clearly spent most of his time in the field. We chatted for about an hour. He told me the Service was allotted a specific amount of money by the state a year, and that didn't include culling coyotes in areas where they were not considered a problem for livestock. His focus was in the farming and ranching areas of the desert. I asked where this extra money was coming from and what his plans were.

"Private sportsmen. They've given us $200,000 extra this year, and possibly want a three-year program. They want us to bait and helicopter cull. In the spring we'll go out on foot into dens."

I told him we've never had Wildlife Services killing coyotes in the mountains, that coyotes aren't a problem in my area, though sometimes random guys come up looking to practice shoot coyotes, but even that's rare. Oddly, Mike seemed sympathetic.

"I like coyotes, they're really smart. The coyotes in the mountains where you live are bigger, healthier, because they aren't harassed by people. Listen, killing coyotes to grow deer isn't going to do anything. Maybe it will save twenty to forty adult deer, out of 2,900. That won't make a difference. Habitat and weather are actually the foremost critical factors in ungulate population numbers. But unfortunately, predators are the low-hanging fruit."

I wondered how they got permissions to snowmobile through a locked area. Mike told me the Forest Service wouldn't have allowed it, but they received permission from the landowner. That way they could bait on her property, and if a coyote ate the meat and went onto Forest Service lands, they could still kill it. He said the meat was from a rendering plant and clean. An additional five locations, some on Game and Fish property, were baited.

"But I can tell you that helicopter burned up a lot of their money and wasn't very successful. We won't do that next year. We only killed about a dozen coyotes, almost all of them on a ranch in the foothills, not in your area."

I told Mike that didn't surprise me. What he was going to encounter in those high meadows were elk. Most of our deer are in the rocky folds of gullies or hanging around the fenced yards of snow-birders' homes.

I still had a lot of unanswered questions. Determined to uncover all the details, with additional phone work, I found that a large portion of the funding came from an organization called the Pennsylvania Bighorn Sheep Association. Not even a Wyoming group of hunters, but big bucks from out of state. The funds were allotted specifically for culling coyotes in hunt zones 106 and 110 where the Game and Fish saw low deer numbers. I was stunned. What this meant was that any organization or individual who came up with the cash can pay Wildlife Services to kill predators even if they are not residents of that state.

May 2019

Within a few months, Game and Fish held a meeting to discuss their upcoming changes to the mountain lion hunt quotas in my zone—the same zone that overlapped with the areas with low deer populations. Every three years, the mountain lion quotas are reviewed, and this year just happened to coincide with the discussions regarding deer. While Game and Fish might not have jurisdiction over coyotes, they do over mountain lions, which are trophy game, meaning they set the hunt quotas and seasons. I had a sinking feeling that the recommendations would raise our quota which was already high at twenty lions and two tags per person. Lions in the state of Wyoming are managed on a source, sink, stable basis. That means how the hunt zones are divided depends upon whether the agency wants to clear lions (a sink population, which might be around populated areas), maintain the population, or provide areas that can foster a source. The entire Absaroka front, mountain lion hunt zone 19, is adjacent to Yellowstone Park, the majority of which is Forest Service lands with a generous amount of wilderness. Thus, I live in a designated source zone.

The meeting was simply informational to discuss wolf and cougar quotas. A few houndsmen were in attendance. Just as I suspected, the recommendations were to increase the quota from twenty to twenty-five lions, but the rationale didn't mention deer. The WGF reasoning was that my hunt area boundaries had been redrawn three years ago (which was true) to exclude the desert, and include the front range of the Absarokas. That way the desert could become a sink zone. After three years, biologists felt there were plenty of cougars within the new boundaries to up the quotas. But clearly, they were under pressure to kill more lions in the hunt area that overlapped with the low deer population.

It was the houndsmen who were objecting. These guys weren't outfitters. They were more interested in running their dogs, getting outdoors, than in killing cougars. Several pointed out that there were few older toms on the landscape. The agency representative acknowledged that, but countered by saying houndsmen could run their dogs into high mountain ridges to find large toms. Of course, lions follow our deer during snow-blanketed months, exactly the months when houndsmen look for tracks. Deer and our elk are lower down, and so are the lions.

Taking a look at the annual tooth aging statistics of killed mountains lions around the state, the houndsmen were correct. Older cats are just not being treed. Successful hunters must bring the skull and pelt to the regional office to be tagged and have an incisor removed. The tooth is aged and the stats are posted yearly. The great majority of cougars for the last three years were aging under five years old, most around two to three years old. That means you have fewer cats living longer and your population isn't thriving. So why would they raise the quotas in a supposed source population? That summer, when the WGF Commission met, the increased mountain lion quota in my area was approved. Whether or not the lion quota was raised solely in an attempt to increase the deer population, deer and elk hunters are quick to blame cougars when these populations crash. And these ungulate hunting tags are what drive the agencies' coffers.

Obviously, there are a lot of factors that control deer populations, weather and habitat probably being the most significant. In a long-term study in Idaho from 1997 to

2003, researchers systematically targeted and removed coyotes and mountain lions. The idea was to test if killing these two predators in particular increased the mule deer population. In one of their control areas, the low doe/fawn ratio was almost identical to my area. The study increased hunting on lions and coyotes, employed Wildlife Services to kill coyotes winter through spring, targeted coyote killing in fawning areas, and decreased human hunting on deer. In other words, it was very intensive as to predator control along with other factors analyzed.

Their results in a nutshell:

Our experimental efforts to change mule deer demography through removal of their two top predators had minimal effects, providing no support for the hypothesis that predator removal would increase mule deer populations. Population growth rates did not increase following predator reduction as predicted.

Winter/Spring 2020

The following winter, Mike abandoned the meat lures and helicopter gunning. The costs couldn't justify the meager results. It was a clear, calm January morning when I picked up my cross-country skis and headed for a remote basin. I was skiing a road, making my own tracks, when a small plane made a few low passes around the nearby field. Wolf collaring here had finished a few weeks ago so this could only be Wildlife Services. Although they were no longer baiting, they were still out looking for coyotes to shoot or at least identify their territories. I saw Mike only one more time during the second year the culling was paid for. It was June and he was driving back to town. We stopped and chatted through our rolled-down windows, Wyoming style, blocking the valley's deserted dirt road. I asked what he was doing.

"Coyote work, up at Self Ridge."

Self Ridge was far up the valley. I sometimes saw wolves running up there in the winter following the elk that coursed the drainages. But snow at Self Ridge is too deep for deer in winter. By now, both he and I knew our migratory deer were working their way into Yellowstone country to fawn. But I liked Mike despite his job and we made conversation for a while.

A few weeks after our vehicle rendezvous, while returning from a hike, I turned up my driveway and was about to open the car door when I noticed a coyote trotting across the field by the forest edge. He set a deliberate pace with something hanging from his mouth. I grabbed my binoculars to see what his prize was. I assumed it was a ground squirrel. To my surprise, he had a fawn in his mouth. The coyote squeezed under the fence, twisting his head to get the fawn through, then darted among the silverberry bushes and disappeared. He was headed to his den site. I decided not to mention the coyote to Mike. He probably would have been amused. He did admire coyotes, their skill, their elusiveness and cunning. He might have even laughed, knowing that with all his hard work he couldn't compete with nature's trickster.

Coyotes will continue to defy man's efforts to exterminate them. After all, in Native legends, coyote was Creator. He was here before humans, and will be here after we are gone. He embodies all our foibles, good and bad. We see our reflection in his exploits. He generously gave humans fire and daylight, but is sometimes portrayed as the embodiment of lechery and evil. He is all of our darkness and our light, at times indiscernible from each other. His indefatigable spirit informs us that in our ineptness, we will never be able to shape wildlife to our needs. Coyote gives us instruction and a road map for the evolution of wildlife agencies.

There have been plenty of articles and books on the futility of Wildlife Services' never-ending killing of coyotes and other wildlife that farmers and ranchers find a nuisance. If killing is the only answer for that industry, then it suggests our human intelligence is but a tiny speck. Using a gun is the least creative solution to any problem. I spent years installing gardens for clients where deer, gophers, moles, and insects were a persistent problem. It affected my financial bottom line just like ranchers or farmers, because if the plants I bought for the homeowner were eaten or died, my guarantee was to replace them for the first season. I didn't just go out and shoot the deer eating my client's roses. I either had to abandon using those tasty plants or come up with creative deterrent solutions.

Wildlife are smart. You can't just use one method for a season and expect it to work every year. Deer teach their fawns what is salad material, gophers change their preferences, and raccoons incessantly unroll new lawns and ground covers to eat the hidden grubs. I have sympathy for people who make their living off the land, but simply picking up the phone for the government wildlife exterminator is lazy and uncreative. Outsmarting wildlife takes ingenuity and hard work, with methods that need to constantly change and adapt.

Killing coyotes to grow deer fits neatly into the unstated mission of wildlife agencies—suppress predator populations to produce more ungulate hunting opportunity. These kinds of decisions are driven by funding sources—hunting and fishing licenses, along with an excise tax on national sales of firearms and ammunition. This model, designed in the early 1900s, worked well initially to support and enhance ungulate species that had been decimated from poaching and market hunting. It evolved from a utilitarian worldview where the natural world was something to be dominated and exploited, and predators (and other wildlife) were competition or nuisance.

Wildlife agencies don't need a mission; they need a new vision. That vision must include approaches that are soundly science-based, holistic, and built around a profound change in their relationship to wildlife and the earth. They need new sources of funding where non-hunters can contribute yet also acquire a seat at the decision-making table. Our job is not to become "farmers of wildlife," but to manage ourselves so that wildlife have space to go about their business of living, procreating, and dying.

After millions of years of co-evolution, in just a few hundred we've forgotten how to act, or even feel, around wildlife. Our brushes with wild nature are reduced to tiny islands of refugia, squeezed between suburbia and freeways, or codified in National Park handouts at campgrounds. We are the same species as our paleolithic ancestors, yet our skills and knowledge of wild animals has shriveled.

If we don't form a new vision for what we call wildlife management, we risk not only losing our sense of communion with wild nature, but losing wild nature altogether. Managing wildlife shouldn't be a knee-jerk response to diverse special interests that have nothing to do with nature's autonomy. Instead, it must give the biota room to breathe without the death knell of being entirely managed, dependent, and farmed.

BIGHORN'S GORDIAN KNOT

San Andres ewe 067 was languishing on a rocky hill-side, chewing on tufts of grass when she heard the far-off noise of a chopper. She hated helicopters. She'd already been netted and captured once. That was when she was four years old. The biologists collared, tested, and treated her for scabies, a disease that was killing her bighorn compadres. During the capture she broke her leg. Although her leg mended, she hadn't forgotten the noise associated with the trauma. Spotting the helicopter in the distance, she darted uphill into a small maze of boulders. The helicopter passed without seeing her.

Before the arrival of the market hunters killing bighorn sheep to feed railroad workers and miners, before settlers trailed thousands of domestic sheep and cattle into Texas and New Mexico, this eighty-five-mile rib of northward trending rock called the San Andres Mountains was prime habitat for desert bighorn sheep. Biologists describe the San Andres and bighorns in nearby mountains as a meta-population: bighorns that travel from one range to another following fluctuations in weather patterns and forage. The home range of ewe 067 probably held the largest population of desert bighorns in the southern Chihuahuan Desert of New Mexico. Unhindered by human interference, bighorns connected north through a desert gap into the Oscura Mountains and southward into the Organ Mountains. With the arrival of livestock that brought diseases, overgrazing, along with unregulated hunting, the bighorns died off. By the 1940s, only a remnant bighorn population lived here.

To save the desert bighorns, the San Andres National Wildlife Refuge was created in 1941. Only thirty-three bighorn sheep remained, mostly in the southern half of the range. White Sands Missile Range was created in 1945, encompassing the Refuge within 3,500 square miles. Seven days later, the first atomic bomb exploded on the northern edge of the military testing site. In a fortuitous quirk of isolation, the Refuge was now surrounded by a huge tract of land, with no public visitation or livestock. The bighorns flourished. The military never used the ground, just the air space, and the bighorns eventually habituated to the screeching sounds of jets and missile launches.

By the mid-1960s, the herd grew to over two hundred bighorn sheep. Yet an isolated population has its limitations, even with high levels of protections from human interference, being subject to genetic drift, disease outbreaks, forage decline, and weather changes. Within the next ten years, by 1979 the herd crashed to around eighty animals and kept declining from there. By the time ewe 067 was born in 1989, only about thirty-five bighorns comprised her herd. The culprit of the crash was determined to be a scabies-mite infestation, its origin a mystery, but the main suspect of transmission was domestic goats and sheep. Scabies causes incessant itching, hair loss, ear drum damage, loss of hearing, and upset equilibrium. The scabies left the bighorns vulnerable to contagious ecthyma, a viral disease that causes scabby lesions on the mouth and can lead to blindness, lameness, impaired feeding, and starvation. This disease complex, if it didn't kill a bighorn outright, predisposes them to death by other causes such as predation, bacterial infections, and falls from precipices.

As seven-year-old ewe 067 hid from the helicopter in the winter of 1996, two other choppers were also surveying the Refuge. In fifteen hours of survey time, not one bighorn sheep was observed. The following year, the concerted effort was repeated, but this time 067 was on a naked bluff. She was captured, collared, and treated for scabies. San Andres ewe 067, the lone remaining native desert bighorn in the Chihuahuan Desert, now became known nationwide as "the last ewe."

San Andres ewe 067 was born on an isolated protected perch with a wide view. Her mother probably sought out rugged terrain for protection from lions, eagles, and coyotes. As the ewe dropped her newborn, an intensive study on mountain lions was taking place within her home range. From 1986 through 1996, Kenneth Logan and Linda Sweanor collared, followed, and documented mountain lions in the Refuge. Bighorn sheep had been listed by the state of New Mexico as endangered in 1980, so although their focus was mountain lions, they agreed to bighorn predation monitoring as well. During the years of the study, the mule deer thrived, so lion kills were mostly opportunistic and compensatory. Of forty-three collared bighorn sheep during their ten-year tenure, twenty-six died, ten from lion kills. Yet after the study was completed, the mule deer population crashed, and mountain lions were hunting farther and wider for food. With the added predation, along with a small, weakened diseased population, all the bighorns disappeared.

All but our last ewe. Ewe 067 watched bighorns around her drop, get eaten by lions, or fall off cliffs while she found safe areas to forage. For two years, 067 lived alone. For a herd animal, she must have become extra vigilant. Ewes in particular like to live high, combing for good escape habitat, a survival instinct honed to protect their lambs. Bighorn sheep have excellent vision. Even at ten years of age, hers must have been highly acute.

Ewe 067 never had much luck with humans. Now easily located with a telemetry collar, during her third capture in 1999, she was placed in a paddock by a guzzler for a week. Bashing her horns against the enclosure, she broke one off.

Possibly 067's luck with humans was about to change. New Mexico Department of Game and Fish (NMDGF) was beginning a new bighorn sheep transplant program. The Refuge with its historical evidence of a large herd of bighorns was on its radar to be next. Yet the scabies transmission was scaring them. How was it communicated—did it stay in the soil? Was it through direct contact? A test was devised to see if the Refuge was safe. The NMDGF brought in six "Sentinel" rams in 1999 from Red Rock Wildlife Refuge, a 1,250-acre fenced enclosure in southwest New Mexico where they were raising bighorn sheep for seed stock. The rams were sprinkled on various ranges, used as canary-in-the-coal-mine bighorns. They waited two years to see if they died. When all the Sentinels lived, additional transplants were brought in from Red Rock, along with bighorns from the Kofa National Wildlife Refuge in Arizona. Between 2001 and 2005, fifty more bighorns were brought in from Kofa along with a few more from Red Rock.

Three years after her capture in the paddock, 067 was spotted with a lamb. One of the Sentinel rams had found her. At thirteen, this feisty survivor had birthed again. She beat a broken leg, scabies, lions, capture, and the terrible fate of aloneness for a herd animal dependent on others.

"Hintza, come!" I'm keeping my ten-month-old golden retriever close. We're walking dry washes in the southern New Mexico Chihuahuan Desert, looking for mule deer, and I just spotted some javelinas on a nearby scrubby slope. Javelinas don't like dogs and have been known to kill them. Really, Lindsay Smythe, my hiking partner, is doing most of the work. I'm just tagging along, holding my recorder out, navigating around creosote bushes and rocky terrain trying to keep up and corral the pup. Smythe is the San Andres Wildlife Refuge manager, here to help her friend and fellow lead biologist Ron Thompson on this four-day project.[1] Smythe points out what javelina scat looks like. "Kind of like cattle droppings." It's everywhere now that I recognize it. Seeing Hintza, the javelinas deposit some fresh scat to confirm.

---

[1] All comments in this essay by Lindsay Smythe are her own opinions and do not represent the U.S. Fish and Wildlife Service.

I was invited to spend a few days on Ted Turner's Armendaris Ranch with a small team of biologists as they completed an annual deer survey. The Armendaris, a desert property bordering the Rio Grande by Elephant Butte Reservoir, is over 350,000 acres of land Turner has reserved for wildlife. It's impressive, a vast swath of private land that stretches across the desert basin east to the San Andres, encompassing much of the Jornada del Muerto, a name given to the basin by the Spanish and known for its waterless expanse. The Fra Cristobal mountains hug the reservoir and western edge of the basin. They're a small range, not terribly high, but their classic crags and high mesas are good bighorn habitat. Looking east, the San Andres appear far in the distance, a long wall of mountains. To the south, much closer, lie the less formidable Caballo mountains, shrouded in clouds suspended above the desert floor.

I'm actually here at the invitation of Ron Thompson, big cat biologist. These days, Thompson mainly spends his time on jaguars in Mexico as president of the Primero Conservation nonprofit. But he still continues his contract work for the Turner Endangered Species Fund. He helped restore these bighorn sheep and continues research for Turner on adaptive mountain lion management strategies, his most recent being water. It was through his work collaring lions on the Kofa that he met Smythe.

Since deer are the primary lion food, it's important to keep tabs on how they are doing with an annual study. Deer health bodes well for bighorn sheep longevity, providing lions with their primary food source. The summer of 2020 was especially hard on all wildlife. The monsoons never arrived. Thompson tells me forage on the ranch is in poor shape.

"The habitat is private land and so the ranch manager is responsible for maintaining healthy habitat. It's not healthy now. We're in a drought and the main browse component is way overused. I'm telling him your plants are dying. And the deer are declining because of the competition."

Thompson points me to a nearby hillside where a series of lines demarcate the slope.

"That's from desert bighorns going back and forth. That used to be all grass. It's been denuded. All been eaten and the bighorns aren't there anymore. Those are the visual impacts I've seen in twenty years of being here. But you can't just come here, look at the mountain, and say, where are the bighorns. They're here and they continue to have an impact."

Thompson says the deer fawn recruitment is down 10%. That's why he's brought this small team to comb, section by section, the Fra Cristobal range. Today, Smythe and I observe one buck, one set of coyote tracks, and several dozen javelina. The bighorns are higher up so we don't expect to see them on this route. Smythe tells me the lower area of the mountain is poor deer country so she's not surprised at our limited success.

Smythe is the perfect person to discuss bighorns and lions with. She's been the sole biologist and manager of the Refuge for two years. Before that, she worked at Kofa National Wildlife Refuge in Arizona, and at the Desert National Wildlife Refuge (DNWR) near Las Vegas, another bighorn refuge surrounded by Nellis Airforce base. Kofa is the main supplier of desert bighorn transplants for Arizona with currently over 900 sheep. The DNWR has 900 bighorns.

Kofa National Wildlife Refuge had a precipitous drop in their bighorn sheep population in the early 2000s, from over eight hundred animals to four hundred. This was before any awareness of the disease complex called *Mycoplasma ovipneumoniae* (Movi). When European settlers brought their domestic sheep and goats throughout the West, those animals carried bacterial diseases for which they had built up immunity over thousands of years. But for native bighorns, these were novel pathogens. Hammered by disease, market hunting, habitat loss, and forage competition, native bighorn populations plummeted. Original numbers throughout the Western states may have been as high as one to two million; by the early 20th century, they were less than twenty-five thousand.

The most obvious approach was to move bighorns from one state to another, from one mountain to another, to wherever bighorns could likely thrive or had existed in the past. Canada was a big exporter. So was Wyoming. It was a well-intentioned mass effort. Unfortunately, though somewhat successful, the efforts only added to the problem. Wildlife managers were simply mixing disease strains all across the West.

Kevin Hurley of the Wild Sheep Foundation describes it to me this way: "The analogy I always use is a daycare. If you put a kid in a room with twenty other snotty-nosed kids, at the end of the day they've swapped about as much spit and goo as they can."

Arizona came particularly late into the disease monitoring game, probably starting only eight years ago. Yet during the early 2000s, this was the situation throughout the West. Bighorn sheep biologists had been chasing diseases for decades, but the science wasn't there yet. Everything was cultured, which is unreliable for identifying and differentiating finicky pathogens.

"We were clueless," Mike Cox of Nevada Department of Wildlife told me. "We didn't want to be clueless, but we didn't have the science behind it. We didn't have any money. Nobody cared. There're no huge grants working on bighorns. We were blind of what was really causing the issue, just a lot of ideas and theories...It was a big circle-jerk for decades."

Then, in 2009, more than two thousand bighorns died throughout the Western states.

"No one understood what was going on. People were thinking it was sunspots," Cox told me, joking to emphasize how blindsided biologists were.

Finally, a breakthrough occurred in the lab. Thomas Besser, a clinical veterinarian pathologist from Washington State University, along with a few others, were able to isolate and identify the ringleader of bighorn bacteria, *Mycoplasma ovipneumoniae* (Movi). Although there are several other bacteria living dormant in bighorns, with their defense mechanisms intact, they can fight those off. But Movi destroys those immunities. Think of Movi as what HIV is to AIDS; it weakens the immune system, leaving it vulnerable to a host of other diseases that might not otherwise kill a bighorn. Biologists call it a "setup artist." The fine hairs in the respiratory tract called ciliary are damaged, the bighorns are coughing, their lungs slowly destroyed. Some develop nasal tumors that make it harder to slough the disease off, becoming super spreaders.

All this was happening sight unseen in the Kofa bighorn die-off in the early 2000s. Since Kofa was providing the majority of the bighorn sheep transplants throughout Arizona, alarm bells went off. Meanwhile, for years, Kofa had been developing more and more artificial water sources specifically for bighorns. In fact, the increase was phenomenal. Arizona had seven hundred fifty managed waters in 1997 for wildlife. By 2019, the state was managing over three thousand. It was through trail cameras set at water developments in the Kofa that managers noticed an increase of mountain lions.

"In that portion of the state, southwestern Arizona, it had very low to no mountain lions historically. A mountain lion might come through, be seen, but it wasn't a regular occurrence." Amber Munig, Big Game Program Management supervisor for Arizona Game and Fish, tells me.

"And we had relatively no mountain lion harvests in that portion of the state for decades. We started to see mountain lions in there, and at one point we had over fourteen mountain lions within the Kofa complex itself."

Arizona Game and Fish sprang into action. Sensitive to public opinion, the agency created a mountain lion predation management plan. They collared bighorns and every mountain lion they could snare. The policy said that if a mountain lion killed two bighorns within a six-month period, that lion was removed. If it only killed one, it was left alone, or if it was two outside of the six months, then it went free.

"We had this very strict approach for dealing with mountain lions killing bighorn sheep," Munig says.

Smythe's employment from 2005 through 2011 at the Kofa coincided with the bighorn drop. She helped push for control limits in their mountain lion management plan. The idea was to target any lions that showed a clear affinity for killing bighorn sheep.

"My opinion is that a lot of the declines (at Kofa) attributed to predation—the real root cause was disease. For a long time, we weren't testing for it at all. When I was at Kofa we had six mountain lions collared, and there were definitely some males that killed a lot of bighorns. There was one that killed six bighorns within the span of a few months. But the problem is every time you had a mountain lion kill a bighorn, it was killed. No one has ever left mountain lions collared long enough to really understand the interaction very well. Everybody starts panicking, and that's what happened in our lion study at Kofa."

Smythe explains that "the intent was to kill offending lions that had really learned how to target bighorn sheep. But it turned out that all the lions met that criteria very quickly and so they ended up killing all of them." It's the rare mountain lion that actually shows a clear preference for one prey or another. Usually, it's an opportunistic kill while hunting for their preferred prey, deer. In Logan and Sweanor's study, only one lion in ten years demonstrated a clear affinity for bighorn sheep. He was removed.

Kofa's predation management plan area was vast. The borders were delineated at Highway 35 to the east, I-10 to the north, I-8 as the southern boundary, and west to the California border. The argument was "you can't just kill lions in the mountain range, because lions migrate in from other places." So potential dispersers were killed too. Because it takes ten to fifteen years for a bighorn herd to rebound from a disease epidemic, it might have eventually cycled out of the infection on its own. It may have happened faster with lion removal, but, as Smythe reiterates, "the problem is they never do research. Everybody starts to panic and the lions always end up losing."

The plan did have a shut-off valve. When the population reached eight hundred, mountain lion killing would end. In 2019, that target population was reached, with over nine hundred animals in the Kofa, thus ending lion culling, a good fifteen years since the plan's inception. The AZGF is still monitoring the collared lions for data purposes, but there is no longer removal of lions.

As we circle around an enormous obstacle of prickly pear cactus, Smythe argues that if every lion is killed in a treatment area, "they have no way of knowing if that's what caused the rebound or not."

Smythe reminds me that in 2002, twenty bighorns were imported into San Andres from the Kofa herd, and another thirty in 2005.

"We know the Kofa decline was caused by disease because when they transplanted the bighorns from Kofa to San Andres, they all came down with Mycoplasma. When we tested them, we strain-typed it, and it's the same strain. It is the Kofa strain that killed my bighorns. All these declines that we've had were more than likely disease. Predation may have compounded that."

Smythe feels the models for bighorn sheep management may be in the San Andres and Desert National Wildlife Refuge. The DNWR has never had lion management, yet they've also had deep disease dips along with rebounds. The San Andres did have a period of state lion controls when the animals were listed as state endangered and reintroduced into the Refuge in the 2000s. An environmental assessment was done and offending lions were to be removed. Over a ten-year period, around thirty lions were culled. But that plan sunsetted and there hasn't been any active lion removal for the last ten years. With the last visual aerial count at one hundred seventy animals, the Refuge population is doing fine, probably around carrying capacity.

In retrospect, game agencies can look back and see the real culprit at the Kofa was Mycoplasma ovipneumoniae. Amber Munig explained it in greater detail.

"What we believe happened is that we had a disease episode that went through the Kofas which affected lamb recruitment and probably an all-age-class die-off. At the same time, we were seeing some expansion of mountain lions, some from south and some from east. We don't know exactly why. Our deer and javelina populations were relatively stable at that time."

"We had predation increasing, something we hadn't had in the past for this population, occurring when the population was depressed. With our predation management and time allowing animals to clear any pathogens that were holding on within the population, it allowed for that population to recover. I think it was a combination of time and our very focused effort to not allow predation to keep suppressing that population."

Yet the question still remains as to why the lion population in the Kofa complex increased from almost zero to those initially observed fourteen animals. Ron Thompson has thoughts on the answer. Along with several other researchers, Thompson conducted a simple, yet elegant long-term study placing camera traps at water catchments spanning all three Southwest deserts—Mohave, Sonoran, and Chihuahuan—including traps in the Kofa. Using data collected over years, the study revealed bighorn sheep using water catchments at limited times of the year, specifically the driest, hottest season. In the Sonoran Desert, where the Kofa traps were located, 85% of all desert bighorn sheep visits occurred during May through August. Bighorns have been evolutionarily adapted to obtain their water from their food. In the winter, they can kick barrel cactus over and chew the pulp. Predators, on the other hand, need year-round water sources. Thompson found "desert bighorn sheep concentrated their visits to water within four to five summer months across all three deserts. Mountain lions, on the other hand, visited water year-round in the Chihuahuan and Mojave deserts, and generally year-round in the Sonoran."

The research concluded that "managed waters allow populations of desert bighorn sheep to inhabit areas they previously had not. Indeed, this outcome forms justification of managing waters for desert bighorn sheep. It follows that managed waters could enable mountain lions to inhabit locations they previously had not..."

Thompson reminds me to "keep this association in mind"—the increase in the number of photos of lions at water developments in the Kofa. "That," meaning the increase in lion numbers, he says, "was suspected as the smoking gun cause for the decline."

Day two of the mule deer survey, I'm out on my own with Hintza. I suppose the researchers feel I've gotten the hang of walking and looking for deer. I'm combing a long wide wash that runs through a deep ravine. Two other volunteers are hiking the high ridges above. I'm assigned to not only look for deer, but scout for lion tracks. Before I set out, Thompson checked a trail camera located on a water source pinch point. No lions had come by.

Although it hasn't rained for weeks, maybe months, a tiny spring emerges through the rough rocks to fill a sandy hole. Hintza gets to quench his thirst. I see javelina tracks everywhere along the sandy bottoms. They resemble small versions of deer tracks set closer together in stride. A few deer tracks, but none in the flesh appear. A large lizard suns itself on the hot rocks. The canyon is stark and beautiful, with gleaming bare stone along the base and sparse desert plants sprinkling the hillsides that rise steeply above.

At one point, I spot Thompson's son who is assisting with the study. A small speck walking along the high rims, sky lining like a bighorn sheep. The canyon opens and ends at a water development with a rough dirt road leading to it. My assignment is to keep walking up the road and connect to another dirt road where we'll all meet. As I've heard so much about water catchments during my time in the Southwest, I spend time studying how this one works.

Thompson told me over last night's dinner how he has applied the data from his research. The idea was to allow bighorns and deer to drink, but not lions. Bighorn sheep and deer have narrow faces; lions have round faces. Those face measurements are known to any researcher. But how long is a lion's tongue? A key question for a cat that can lap through bars. Since Thompson spends a lot of time capturing and collaring lions, it was just one additional measurement. The design he came up with was a trough with pipe laid vertically just wide enough for a lean bighorn nose, and water depth just beyond a lion's tongue reach. Water for thirsty deer and bighorns, yet a deterrent for lions in waterless country. If water isn't available, lions and other predators will have to search far and wide, leaving the bighorns, who are less water-dependent, alone.

That predators kill prey is the simplest of biological equivalents, known to any high-schooler. But the intricate dance of nature is a puzzle that humans have difficulty teasing out even absent our interference. Yet nature has been so tinkered with, trampled on, and altered by humans, that when one adds our own unintended consequences to the fluidity of natural factors like climate, habitat, and disease, sorting out cause becomes a veritable soup. To save an animal from extinction, we now find it necessary to trade wildness for rescue interventions.

"Watch this," Ron Thompson says. He was driving back to the research bungalow on the Armendaris Ranch when he spotted a half dozen oryx hanging by the side of the road near a fence line. We'd stopped to watch them as they nonchalantly eyed us back. Huge, bulky, like a hefty elk with forty-inch scimitar-shaped horns, their beautiful and unusual black and white facial pattern reminded me of a Rorschach test. A black triangle framed their noses with mirrored white splotches on either side. With sharp black-edged body markings and tan bodies, oryx have a regal exotic appearance. The animals stood and stared at the truck, just a few feet away.

"They love to race trucks. As soon as we start, they'll run, then cut across us."

My pup Hintza was in the back seat. I called to alert him to what was about to take place. As Ron gunned the truck, the oryx take off. Hintza had a happy moment watching them run, his head out the window. But the oryx don't speed off into the horizon like the pronghorn I'm used to in Wyoming. They quickly get bored and resume standing and staring from the opposite side of the road.

Oryx, also known as gemsbok, were brought here in the late 1960s. Frank Hibben, avid big game hunter, controversial archaeologist, professor at University of New Mexico, and chairman of the New Mexico Game and Fish Commission, had the bright idea of bringing oryx in for a big game hunting experience. To hunters, the barrenness of the Missile Range must have appeared as if it needed filling up. Researchers believed they'd simply stay within the Tularosa Basin, never growing beyond five hundred to six hundred animals. Mountain lions would control them, they said. But in Africa, prides of lions hunt them. Our solitary lions would rather take their chances on smaller, less formidable prey.

Ninety-three oryx were brought to the Missile Range between 1969 and 1973. Oryx barely need water, they eat anything with or without leaves, have no natural predators, and breed year-round. Instead of self-limiting, the oryx thrived. The Land of Enchantment was now theirs for the overtaking. Six thousand today roam in southern New Mexico, and they need more and more room. Oryx inhabit not just the dry basins, but wander through mule deer and bighorn sheep habitat, stand on bajadas, invade washes, intrude on private lands, and comingle with bighorn sheep.

Lindsay Smythe tells me the San Andres Refuge allows depredation hunts from September through March. Hunters are escorted to the field, and told which one to shoot. Males have harems and the animals are difficult to sex.

Smythe is also concerned about disease transfer. "I will tell you on our bighorn sheep survey, I saw a lot of oryx up in bighorn country. I started to count them, but finally gave up. We're going to burn up too much fuel (in the helicopter) counting oryx instead of bighorn. They don't get up into the highest steepest areas, but they do definitely interact."

She wonders if the scabies outbreak that brought the bighorns almost to extinction in the 1990s might not have been transferred from oryx. The timeline certainly fits, with precipitous drops in the bighorn population around ten years after the oryx introduction. Even so, the Refuge still has issues with other diseases common to bighorns, which oryx definitely do transmit. Plus, scientists are still learning about the entire disease complex in bighorn sheep transmissible from other ungulates, including cattle.

Even with over a thousand hunt tags issued every year, the NMGF can't keep the oryx in check.

Nearby, on the Turner Armendaris Ranch, biologists are concerned about over-browsing due to oryx. The ranch holds oryx hunts every year, with reduced rates in the Fra Cristobals, bighorn country. Turner has one of the largest bighorn herds in New Mexico. The browse pressure from oryx compounds other thorny problems like drought and climate change.

Over in Nevada, a similar problem exists but with a more recognizable species. Nevada once held the largest desert bighorn population in the West. The state's classic basin-range topography was considered one huge metapopulation. When I asked Mike Cox about his biggest concern, he said "if you love wildlife in Nevada, the biggest problem that should be on the top of your to-do list is feral horses. We have more biomass of wild feral horses than the combined wild ungulate populations in the state of Nevada." I asked Cox where those horses were concentrated. Were they in bighorn country?

"They're everywhere. They're in the Mohave Desert, they're in the Great Basin Desert, they're in the sub-alpine, they're in the alpine."

"How many horses do you have?"

"About 60,000. Way too many cows, way too many horses. Our ecosystem is being destroyed as we speak. (Nevada) is going to be unable to move into the future if you overlay climate change."

Even when I asked him about Nevada's policies on mountain lion controls for bighorns, his response was telling.

"We shut a couple of bighorn herd hunts down, not because of disease, but because of lion predation *and* (Cox's emphasis) feral horses."

When I thought he was speaking solely of habitat destruction, he corrected me.

"They drink all the water. A bighorn will never go back to a water source that has a horse, ever. It's their behavior. Because of that, they get hugely impacted and die of thirst as the horses guard the water source for four months of the year."

Cox segued into mountain lions and water sources. "When they have to go to a water source, mountain lions have such a great learned behavior and very efficient, so they can take their toll on the population. Mountain lions are not the reason that bighorns are in trouble, just the tip of the spear. There are a lot of things that contribute to bighorns not doing well."

I'm in Tucson for the month of December, staying in a rental house nestled along the base of the Santa Catalina mountains. In years past, I've explored Tucson's general area, but I've never had a prolonged stay within the city proper.

Tucson has a beautiful backdrop. Besides being cradled by the Santa Catalinas, which rise up to 9,000 feet, its eastern border is Saguaro National Park East, and its western border is the National Park West. Other smaller sky islands dot Tucson's surroundings. The foothills of the Catalinas are filled with stately saguaro cactus, like tall multi-armed soldiers guarding the mountain itself. The main two-lane artery, Catalina Scenic Highway, pushes ever upward through numerous ecosystems, from desert scrub through pine-oak woodlands and finally to Mt. Lemmon and a subalpine forest. The mountain, so close to a city of half a million people, is a playground for recreationists. What stood out for me amidst the beauty of the landscape was the development that's skyrocketing. Trophy homes and golf courses clasp the edges right up to the public lands. Suburbia surrounds the National Park. The desert floor is a sea of traffic and homes between the surrounding mountain ranges.

Desert bighorn sheep once roamed freely from range to range across the desert floor. This allowed the bighorns to search for precious water sources, food, and escape habitat from predators. The Santa Catalinas can only support about one hundred twenty bighorns, a tiny population vulnerable to genetic decline, drought, and disease. But with connections to other populations in surrounding ranges, these bighorns could exchange genetics, ensuring their survival. Walk-abouts are built into the hard-wiring of bighorn sheep, in particular males, for this very reason.

This scenario was what populated the Sky Islands of southern Arizona for thousands of years with bighorn sheep. Yet like throughout the West, market hunting, livestock diseases, and habitat destruction caused the bighorn population to plummet. Still, they persisted in the Catalinas while other nearby ranges winked out.

Joe Sheeley grew up in Tucson. As a boy, he watched bighorns on the mountains, fascinated with their agility, spryness, and ability to negotiate even the toughest terrain. But by 1996, the Catalina bighorn herd disappeared. The Arizona Game and Fish department was sending biologists to Pusch Ridge, the favorite escape haunts of the bighorns, to periodically scout for them, yet they always came up empty. New rules were created with the hope if there were bighorns they could be protected: no dogs on Pusch Ridge trails, no hiking off-trail during lambing season. Yet no lambs, rams, or ewes were ever seen.

Sheeley is the former Arizona Desert Bighorn Sheep Society president. With the influx of new disease science, in hindsight he has his own theory of what happened.

"In the late 1980s, a ram made it all the way from the Superstitions to the Catalinas."

"The Superstitions are east of Phoenix. That's a long trek," I commented.

"Bighorn sheep that had been transplanted from the Kofa mountain range to the Canyon Lake Superstition area had yellow ear tags. That's how we know where the ram came from. In my opinion, there is no telling what that ram came into contact with in his journey to the Catalinas. I really believe he ran across hobby domestic sheep or goats, and I think that herd got infected with disease and died off very quickly."

In the 1970s and 1980s, game agencies, fueled by money and demand from hunting groups along with the awareness of the steep losses of bighorns across the West, began intensively translocating Rocky Mountain and Desert bighorns into their once native ranges. Arizona Game and Fish (AZGF) was no exception. Ramping up reintroductions across the state, they had done extensive evaluations of historical ranges along with habitat features. Although the Catalinas were of highest quality habitat, the mountain was put on the back burner for relocations.

AZGF had been doing relocations in low-density population areas where people didn't care or pay attention to their predator management policies. Clearing lions prior to a reintroduction wouldn't fly in the progressive, environmentally minded city of Tucson. Even the agency's somewhat scaled-down predator policy for the Kofas would be highly controversial. The agency had to figure out a way to gain the public's trust in order to put bighorns back on the mountain.

Munig told me: "The Catalinas were unique because it is next to a large metropolitan area. And we knew there would be a lot of interest in how we would approach it and a lot of controversy in any kind of predation management we were to implement."

The mountain lion population in the Catalinas was quite healthy. Based on hunt data and field data prior to the project, AZGF estimated sixty-seven mountain lions on the mountain. But the Catalinas had healthy herds of deer, coatis, and javelinas.

To the agency's credit, they embarked on a bold idea—a working group comprised of a variety of stakeholders. They pledged to abide by the group's plan, which would be adaptive depending upon any change in conditions. Four environmental groups opted in, including the Center for Biological Diversity and Sky Island Alliance. On the other side were sportsmen, Arizona Game and Fish, and Arizona Desert Bighorn Sheep Society. Disagreement abounded, but the biggest rift was the mountain lion strategy. As one might imagine, opinions ranged from doing no predator controls to clearing the mountain of lions in advance of translocations.

Reintroductions of bighorn sheep are typically done in three to four rounds of thirty bighorns. A small herd of thirty bighorns, neophytes to a new habitat, devoid of any resident bighorns that can guide them to prime escape habitat, are exceptionally vulnerable to predation. In previous translocations, AZGF usually took what they considered the safest, and easiest, way to give new introductions a leg up by "pre-treating" the area and raising lion quotas. By committing to an advisory board consensus, a middle ground was ensured. Every bighorn would be collared instead of the customary one out of every three bighorns. No lions would be collared. Lions would be pursued and killed only after evidence showed they'd killed a bighorn, and the pursuit was to be cut off after five days. Females with kittens would be off-limits. Mortalities would be identified through their GPS signal and only then would a pursuit be triggered. This was a complete turnabout to the Kofa plan where every lion in a wide net surrounding the refuge was collared, which made tracking and dispatching easy.

The first capture and translocation took place in November of 2013. Thirty-one bighorns—seven rams and twenty-four ewes—were released. By the end of March 2014, sixteen bighorns were dead, fourteen by lions. Because of the difficult terrain and the policy of no lion collaring, only three lions had been removed. Houndsmen had to run the lion off a kill to identify the offending lion. One lion went down a cliff face, too steep for the dogs to pursue. Some went into developed areas so the chase was called off. Even with the sheep predation plan transparent and publicized, the steep losses produced a public outcry on all sides. At a packed Game and Fish public meeting, protesters showed up holding signs.

"We went out of the way to make sure the public knew what we were up to," said Randy Serraglio of the Center for Biological Diversity. "People tend to not pay attention to something like that until there's a dead lion. Then everybody is keenly interested."

Everyone had expected some losses, but losing half the bighorns was a shock. With the GPS collars in place, managers could visualize where the bighorns were moving. Sheeley says the first release site was based on his historic observations, but many of the bighorns, unfamiliar with the mountain, headed for the high forests. Without clear visibility, good escape habitat, and naivete as to their bearings, they were easy pickings for lions. Luckily, the remaining bighorn sheep found the prime habitat of Pusch Ridge. There they thrived. In fact, at least five lambs were born in the spring with the herd stabilizing. No mortalities were observed for the next seven months. The advisory board had stood firm in their consensus on lions, even in the heat of controversy. With the good news, the second release was scheduled for November and another thirty bighorn sheep. This time, using their generational genetic compass, those bighorns headed for their kin right up to Pusch Ridge. Two more releases took place through 2016.

Mark Hart, public information officer for AZGF, tells me what he felt happened was some of the bighorns came from mountain ranges where no lions existed.

"Most of the bighorn sheep came from the Yuma area, but one year we did take one-half of the allotment from the Superstition mountains. Those bighorns did not fare well. One reason is they did not have prior exposure to pneumonia and a few of them got it and died. You can't prove this scientifically, but what we felt was also happening was they were not as well adapted to the presence of lions as the Yuma-area ones were. So the lions picked off a few."

By the end of the project, eight lions were taken out over the four years of the relocation project. The Catalinas may be a model of how these relocations should be conducted. If there hadn't been an advisory board representing a wide variety of voices, it's almost certain AZGF would have resorted to clearing the area of lions before a second release commenced. As of fall 2020, seventy-five bighorns were on the mountain, with the predator program retired in 2016. Lamb recruitment is almost 50% (typical is 25%), with many sightings of uncollared rams and ewes, indicating they were born on the mountain. Since the mountain only historically supported about one hundred twenty big-horns, the Catalina bighorn herd is well on its way to success.

Even so, the future of the Catalina herd is uncertain. That herd, along with others on isolated ranges in the desert Southwest, face a myriad of problems. One of the biggest unknowns is the consequences bighorns will face with climate change and the drying of the West.

One of the biggest stumbling blocks biologists confront is bighorn sheep connectivity. Rams, looking for mates and to spread their genetics, do walk-abouts, usually in circles encompassing thirty to forty miles. Even if they begin their journey healthy, they might run into domestic lambs or goats, contract the disease, then bring it back to their herd. One ram came from Colorado into southern Wyoming, traveling over four hundred miles and through three different bighorn herds. Wyoming Game and Fish only knew this because the ram was collared, and they were alerted by Colorado Parks and Wildlife. Bighorns are gregarious—sheep like sheep. They don't need to touch noses to get infected. They might even be kilometers away if the wind is right. Because Wyoming Game and Fish had no idea if this ram came into contact with domestic stock, be it a large herd or a hobby rancher, they couldn't take a chance. This one ram could cost hundreds of sheep lives and devastate entire herds. The ram was euthanized.

Sky Islands and basin/range topography are comprised of isolated islands of habitat. Minimal population size for healthy genetic diversity seems to be around two hundred animals to ward off most stressors. Historically, when desert bighorns existed as metapopulations, bighorns could roam and connect freely. A bighorn population wasn't just one mountaintop, but a wide swath of desert and mountains containing sub-populations inside of metapopulations. Research biologist Harley Shaw commented to me that in looking at the history of desert bighorns in the Southwest, his view was that, historically, mountain ranges with these small populations were constantly winking out. Roaming instincts would push a few bighorns across desert floors to repopulate new ranges. Today that's a near impossibility.

I asked Mike Cox about connectivity today in Nevada. "It's pretty sad, especially in Clark County, which is the county of Las Vegas. We have islands, these sky islands of bighorn sheep that can't go anywhere. They can't roam. They can't go on forays or they'll get killed on six- or eight-lane highways."

Roads, fences, housing developments, and domestic livestock are among the many obstacles bighorns face for genetic connectivity. Without a viable solution, many wildlife agencies resort to periodic infusions of additional bighorns on a mountain. With new knowledge of disease strains, even that has its limitations. AZGF was looking to boost a bighorn sheep population southwest of the Colorado River. They tested both herds and although both have titers for Mycoplasma ovipneumoniae, the strains were different so they canceled the translocation.

Other solutions are more drastic. In 2015, in the Tendoy Mountains southwest of Bozeman, Montana Department of Fish, Wildlife, and Parks sold 311 hunt tags for any bighorn in an area with only thirty animals. Drawing a bighorn ram tag in any Western state is like winning the lottery. Many hunters apply year after year, yet never draw a tag in their lifetime. But this fall in Montana was different, because the Tendoy herd had been struggling for years. Movi was causing die-offs and low lamb recruitment. The heart-breaking solution the department devised was to eliminate the entire herd and start anew. Any bighorns hunters didn't kill, the department would. Five years later, in 2020, the department announced they'd begin transplanting bighorns into the Tendoys again.

Mike Cox is looking toward another solution. Some of the new research points to chronic asymptomatic disease shedders as the reason why a herd just cannot recover. The newest push is to find these shedders and kill them, called "test and remove." Experiments in Oregon's Hells Canyon by researcher Francis Cassirer show promising results with a natural fade-out of the disease over time when carriers were removed in connected populations. But, as Cox points out to me, "just because one bighorn gets one Mycoplasma strain doesn't mean the next strain that comes along won't be worse. There is no immunity that's generated from one to the other."

Jessica Moreno, with the Coalition for Sonoran Desert Protection, looks to wildlife linkages as a viable solution for healthy wildlife. Focusing mainly on Pima County around the Greater Tucson area, the Coalition partnered with Arizona Department of Transportation and others to plan wildlife crossings. The first completed crossing was an underpass and overpass along State Route 77 installed in 2016. This first of several planned crossings would eventually allow passage from the Catalinas over Interstate 10, through several island ranges and west into the Tohono O'odham Nation Reservation.

Moreno's viewpoint is that bighorns face a tangled web of stressors, and many we might not even understand or recognize as stressors. But if we look at the bigger picture, giving the bighorns room to connect, even if one population crashes, more bighorns will come in to boost the population. So far, no bighorn sheep have been observed using the State Route 77 crossing, although crossings elsewhere have been successful for bighorns. Wildlife crossings installed between Kingman and the Nevada state line on U.S. 93 documented use in the first four years by over six thousand bighorns. Given the complexity of disease issues, it's hard to know if these kinds of connections might provide the fresh genetic flow, yet doom a population to new strains of disease.

The biggest unknown of all is our rapidly changing climate. Connective corridors undoubtedly help facilitate movement, allowing wildlife to adjust to habitat changes and water availability as their environment heats up. The totality of all the issues affecting bighorn sheep in particular is complicated and nuanced. Connective corridors might solve one piece of their Gordian knot but certainly not all.

I grab my snowshoes, prepare a few snacks, and head up to a high mesa locals call Little Bald Ridge. In deep snow it's difficult to follow the spines of the lower ravines that lead to the mountaintop and the animal trail that hugs the hillside higher up would be obscured. But we've had little snow this winter and today with a clear sky, a light wind, and temperatures in the teens, it should only take an hour to climb to the wide butte.

I'm hoping to see our little band of Rocky Mountain bighorn sheep. They like the windswept meadows and craggy overlooks. The elk covet the area too, though the two species never group up. Wolves might be there, but their interest is in the scent of the elk, not the bighorns.

The final ascent leaves me a bit winded. The trees have disappeared. I always have to remember to watch for a large sinkhole beside the animal route where the trail swings directly alongside. The elk have trodden down the snow by its edges, but the hole is steep and deep and makes me nervous. I climb the last few hundred yards to the meadow expanse. The ground is cropped clean from the large elk herds who take advantage of this high windy spot that sweeps the snow clear. Even the sagebrush is just bare stems. As I clear the rise, I spot the sheep. A small band of ewes and lambs clasp the rocky cliff edges along the eastern rim. The meadows stretch to the west in a large expanse. Picking up my binoculars, I see a mixed age group of rams grazing in a hollow below.

I've been here before in winter without seeing bighorn sheep or elk. The wind is usually in a howl, which highlights those moments of deep terrestrial loneliness. Without the bighorns, this top-of-the-world is not right. It's definitely special to see them here today. Even so, these small groupings evoke both elation and sadness. I know that on these same ridges, just a few hundred years ago, the native peoples who lived in these mountains watched herds of hundreds, perhaps thousands, of bighorns. These are the hanger-oners, the bighorn sheep that survived the onslaught of white men and their livestock diseases. They are the toughest, yet they eye me with sweet docility, unafraid of my presence. I sit down a few hundred yards away and enjoy. Soon they pay me no mind, and go about their browsing business.

Bighorn sheep appear tough because of the rugged places they live, yet in reality they are soft creatures, whether we are speaking of their animal nature or their constitution. Just being with them I feel softer. I'd like my grandchildren to be able to experience their soft-tough nature. The fact that their presence on this planet coincides with ours implies we must care about their plight, not let it extinguish. That requires us to answer difficult ethical and moral questions. First, there is the money that supports these herculean efforts to help bighorns. We're talking about millions of dollars. Only one-quarter of all state game agency revenues comes from bighorn hunting licenses sold to the public. The other three-quarters comes from governor's auctions and raffles. Kevin Hurley of the Wild Sheep Foundation gives me an example.

"In South Dakota, by statute, there are only two bighorn sheep licenses and they are resident only. That generates $550 a year in revenue. The first year they had [a governor's tag], it sold for $102,000, and 100% of it went back to South Dakota Game, Fish and Parks. So for $102,000 think what can you do for bighorn sheep versus $550."

Very few bighorn hunting tags are sold per state every year. The situation with bighorns is just too precarious. What supports bighorn programs are these auctioned tags, bought by the super wealthy. For instance, Rick Smith, a retired telecommunications executive from Dallas, was the highest bidder in New Mexico's auction and won seven tags over eight consecutive years to hunt bighorn sheep. He spent over $1 million on those tags, 90% of which goes directly to New Mexico Game and Fish's bighorn sheep enhancement program.

If we value bighorn sheep, then there needs to be a way to fund programs that support bighorns other than through hunts and super tags. There is something obscene in the sole financial support to save bighorns throughout the West—native wildlife that are in the public trust—relying on a sliver of mega-rich trophy hunters. Additionally, being dependent exclusively on hunters for bighorn dollars creates a vicious cycle that pressures agencies to put more bighorns on every mountain so as to increase revenue. It also fuels extreme predator management programs like in New Mexico, where the culling of lions never ends despite bighorn herds that are thriving.

Funding is only one aspect. I think we have to be honest—the intensity of desert bighorn life-support programs may soon be beyond justification. We need to ask ourselves the hard questions. Can we continue to transport water, not only because of the price tag, but as water itself becomes more precious in a thirsty Southwest, will the program even be sustainable? With the extreme drought conditions of 2020, Arizona hauled close to one million gallons of water, some even by helicopter, to catchments for bighorns especially as well as other wildlife.

Mycoplasma ovipneumoniae is here for the long run. Researchers are still puzzled as to how to control it and its emerging new strains. If we support separation of bighorns from domestic sheep and goats, are we willing to boycott wool from Western wool growers? Or to contribute cash to buy out wool growers and their public lands grazing allotments? While bighorn sheep NGOs have already been actively raising dollars to help retire grazing allotments, isn't this the responsibility of all Americans? Again, wildlife are in the public trust, therefore all of our responsibility.

It's obviously absurd and expensive to keep plopping new bighorn sheep recruits into mountain ranges to enhance their gene flow. Should we instead adopt the "test and remove" program, where shedders are identified and culled? Do we give this kind of program a cut-off limit?

There is a point sometime in the future where we'll have to cut bighorns loose. Yet we do have an obligation to the bighorns to do our best for them, to right so many of the wrongs they've suffered from our misdeeds. In my mind, perhaps *our best* is displayed in places like the Desert National Wildlife Refuge in Nevada or San Andres National Wildlife Refuge—immense tracts of mountain ranges surrounded by even larger tracts of wild areas completely off-limits to the public and livestock. Allow the bighorn populations to fluctuate naturally.

Instead of trying to fill every historically occupied mountain with bighorn sheep, we should consider a sub-population model, where suitable habitat can provide the bighorns natural connective corridors to other nearby ranges. Land might need to be purchased to enlarge the protected area and grazing allotments retired. Initial habitat restoration would be completed, then we'd just let bighorns be bighorns, and lions be lions. This would be asking a lot of the general public; we all need to step up, not just hunters and the super-rich who can buy tags. An egalitarian effort is needed, an extreme push, perhaps a sprint rather than a marathon. For the bighorn's sake, it's time to decide if we are all willing to rise up to the task this implies—to be guardians of the ancient way of life of the bighorn sheep. At the very least, we owe it to the bighorns to take a hard look at ourselves and what we are willing to do.

Acknowledgments

I n order to complete the research for Bighorn's Gordian Knot, I conducted numerous interviews. Special thanks to Amber Munig along with Rana Tucker and Mark Hart of Arizona Game and Fish for taking time out of their busy workdays. Joe Sheeley, Ricardo Small, and Jessica Moreno also contributed to my understanding of the Santa Catalina bighorn relocation. Thanks to Caitlin Ruhl, biologist with New Mexico Game and Fish, who answered my desert bighorn questions. Kevin Hurley of The Wild Sheep Foundation is the bearer of all bighorn knowledge. Doug McWhirter of Wyoming Game and Fish has spent his life working with and understanding bighorns and walked me through the history of bighorns in the Absarokas. Mike Cox of Nevada Department of Wildlife was a wealth of insight about disease as well as bighorn status in Nevada and California. Thanks to Mead Dominick who knows Rocky Mountain bighorns because he is out there in the field with them. Lindsay Smythe and Ron Thompson both gave me the working biologists' perspective on bighorns and mountain lions.

I also want to send my appreciation out to biologists at Wyoming Game and Fish, Dan Thompson and Ken Mills, who always amicably respond to my tough questions on wolves and cougars. Also, Kerry Murphy of Shoshone National Forest and retired biologist Joe Harper helped with my lynx inquiries.

Thank you, Harley Shaw, for critiquing my bighorn essay. He is a special friend who has deep working knowledge of all things wild.

ABOUT THE AUTHOR

L eslie Patten is a naturalist with a background in landscape design and environmental sustainability, complemented with extensive romping in wilderness. Her most recent journalistic foray is a children's book entitled *Koda and the Wolves* for grades three to six. She presently lives in a small cabin in northwest Wyoming.